Portable
Faith

More praise for *Portable Faith:*

Our churches are filled people who want to live out the way of Jesus in their neighborhoods and cities—and especially among "the least of these." But amidst the complexity, changing landscape, and increasing fragmentation in our society, many of us don't feel qualified or simply don't know where to start. Sarah Cunningham offers wise perspective, hopeful stories, and practical steps so that faith communities can be equipped to make a difference. *Portable Faith* manages to combine the best thinking on missional theology and community engagement with tangible tools for leaders.

—Mark Scandrette, husband, father, teacher, activist, and author of *Practicing the Way of Jesus* and *FREE: Spending Your Time and Money on What Matters Most*

With gentle wisdom and penetrating insight, Sarah Cunningham has given us a great gift in *Portable Faith*—a gift that has the capacity to cause a seismic shift in the way churches understand what it means to "into all the world." Incredibly practical and viable in its exercises and ideas, and equally profound in philosophy and rationale, this book has the power to revolutionize congregations from the inside out and transform the communities they serve.

—Karla Yaconelli, former managing editor of *The (Wittenburg) Door* and formerly the co-owner of Youth Specialties

A lot of folks today, inside and outside of the church, recognize there's a problem with how we're doing things. The going-out-into-the-world we read about in the pages of the Gospels is all but missing in our local congregations. We *want* to be the church differently, but we don't know how. *Sarah Cunningham knows how.* If you want to mobilize people to engage the community in which you're situated, to change and be changed, *Portable Faith* is the primer you need.

—Margot Starbuck, author of *Small Things with Great Love: Adventures in Loving Your Neighbor,* www.MargotStarbuck.com

More praise for *Portable Faith:*

Our churches are filled people who want to live out the way of Jesus in their neighborhoods and cities—and especially among "the least of these." But amidst the complexity, changing landscape, and increasing fragmentation in our society, many of us don't feel qualified or simply don't know where to start. Sarah Cunningham offers wise perspective, hopeful stories, and practical steps so that faith communities can be equipped to make a difference. *Portable Faith* manages to combine the best thinking on missional theology and community engagement with tangible tools for leaders.

—Mark Scandrette, husband, father, teacher, activist, and author of *Practicing the Way of Jesus* and *FREE: Spending Your Time and Money on What Matters Most*

With gentle wisdom and penetrating insight, Sarah Cunningham has given us a great gift in *Portable Faith*—a gift that has the capacity to cause a seismic shift in the way churches understand what it means to "into all the world." Incredibly practical and viable in its exercises and ideas, and equally profound in philosophy and rationale, this book has the power to revolutionize congregations from the inside out and transform the communities they serve.

—Karla Yaconelli, former managing editor of *The (Wittenburg) Door* and formerly the co-owner of Youth Specialties

A lot of folks today, inside and outside of the church, recognize there's a problem with how we're doing things. The going-out-into-the-world we read about in the pages of the Gospels is all but missing in our local congregations. We *want* to be the church differently, but we don't know how. *Sarah Cunningham knows how.* If you want to mobilize people to engage the community in which you're situated, to change and be changed, *Portable Faith* is the primer you need.

—Margot Starbuck, author of *Small Things with Great Love: Adventures in Loving Your Neighbor*, www.MargotStarbuck.com

More praise for *Portable Faith*:

Our churches are filled people who want to live out the way of Jesus in their neighborhoods and cities—and especially among "the least of these." But amidst the complexity, changing landscape, and increasing fragmentation in our society, many of us don't feel qualified or simply don't know where to start. Sarah Cunningham offers wise perspective, hopeful stories, and practical steps so that faith communities can be equipped to make a difference. *Portable Faith* manages to combine the best thinking on missional theology and community engagement with tangible tools for leaders.

—Mark Scandrette, husband, father, teacher, activist, and author of *Practicing the Way of Jesus* and *FREE: Spending Your Time and Money on What Matters Most*

With gentle wisdom and penetrating insight, Sarah Cunningham has given us a great gift in *Portable Faith*—a gift that has the capacity to cause a seismic shift in the way churches understand what it means to "into all the world." Incredibly practical and viable in its exercises and ideas, and equally profound in philosophy and rationale, this book has the power to revolutionize congregations from the inside out and transform the communities they serve.

—Karla Yaconelli, former managing editor of *The (Wittenburg) Door* and formerly the co-owner of Youth Specialties

A lot of folks today, inside and outside of the church, recognize there's a problem with how we're doing things. The going-out-into-the-world we read about in the pages of the Gospels is all but missing in our local congregations. We *want* to be the church differently, but we don't know how. *Sarah Cunningham knows how.* If you want to mobilize people to engage the community in which you're situated, to change and be changed, *Portable Faith* is the primer you need.

—Margot Starbuck, author of *Small Things with Great Love: Adventures in Loving Your Neighbor*, www.MargotStarbuck.com

Portable Faith

How to Take Your Church to the Community

Sarah Cunningham

Abingdon Press
Nashville

PORTABLE FAITH
HOW TO TAKE YOUR CHURCH TO THE COMMUNITY

Copyright © 2013 by Abingdon Press

All rights reserved.

This book is printed on acid-free paper.

Library of Congress Cataloging-in-Publication Data

Cunningham, Sarah Raymond, 1978-
Portable faith : how to take your church to the community / by Sarah Cunningham.
      pages cm
   ISBN 978-1-4267-5515-6 (pbk. : alk. paper) 1. Communities—Religious aspects—Christianity. 2. Church work. 3. Evangelistic work. I. Title.
   BV625.C86 2013
   253'.7—dc23

                                                                  2012050149

13 14 15 16 17 18 19 20 21 22—10 9 8 7 6 5 4 3 2 1

MANUFACTURED IN THE UNITED STATES OF AMERICA

To Westwinds Community Church,
who nurtured me through my most zealous days
and gave me the freedom to chase inspired ideas;

Rivertree Community Church,
who humbly embodies love for its surrounding community
and endeavors to embrace the act of going;

And a gracious, generous God, who completes what he starts,
who set a young girl on a platform she didn't deserve,
and who, in time, allowed the compassion that grew in her heart to
find the wisdom necessary to produce a healthier and broader telling
of what she learned along the way.

True godliness does not turn men out of the world, but enables them to live better in it and excites their endeavors to mend it.

—*William Penn*

Contents

An Invitation

This is a book about *living* and *being* church.

It's about freeing God (or rather our perceptions of Him) from the bars of a sixty-minute service and a Sunday prison. And about using sanctuary seat time to catapult our belief beyond the four walls of the church building.

The coming pages, then, are an invitation for congregations to seek God in the open air, to embody Jesus in the streets, and to carry faith into the six days and twenty-three hours between Sunday worship services.

It's a charge to indulge in first-century wisdom and to join the historic band of believers whose participation in "church" seemed surgically stitched to the way they lived their faith in the public sphere.

To remember together that as Jesus abides in us and we in him, our presence in our communities reveals an important reality to our culture:

Jesus is still on the move.

Acknowledgments

With special thanks to Paul Nemecek, Wayne Gordon, Jim Henry, Oreon Trickey, Rick Lee, and Sean Young, who engaged me in meaningful experiences that expanded my understanding of community.

To Edward Flanigan, David Wilkinson, Ray Bakke, Ron Sider, Jim Wallis, John Perkins, David Clarebaut, Gerald Schlabach, and the people behind Covenant House, whose writings influenced the thoughts that informed my young intentions.

To Lil, Len, Constance, Hampton, and others at Abingdon who gave me the opportunity to invite others into this story.

To Ron, Scott, Norma, Amy, Taryn, Ed, Cammie, Kat, and Dave, who endured the growing pains of my fledgling attempts to save the world with grace.

And once again, to my family, especially to my father, who still advances the cause of Christ as a church planter.

Lastly, to my husband, the Emperor Justus, and Malachi, his newly appointed Chief of Staff, who are my closest community in this world.

Who This Book Is For

This book is for pastors, church staff, and elders seeking practical ideas that encourage their congregations outward, without suggesting attenders abandon the churches in which they have staked their lives. It's for church leaders who need a hybrid tool that respects the delicate balancing act of being both a church that calls people to come and a church that is willing to get up and go.

It's for professors and students who are neck deep in spiritual formation, who've realized that the best ministry and seminary courses must have a lived-out component. It's for those who rightly worry that having correct doctrine on paper, but failing to embody those beliefs in practice, is an accidental but dangerous heresy.

It's for those wandering nomads who feel most comfortable outside the church, and those lovely, crazy zealots who find the best visions of God in soup kitchens and on mountain hikes, in protests on Capitol Hill or in the lyrics of a folk song.

It's for tradition lovers, institution haters, and the often undefined groups of the religious and irreverent in between.

It's for anyone willing to get his or her hands dirty in the work of Jesus.

The call to a *going*, portable faith rises from the New Testament world, from Jesus' parting instructions to his disciples, and connects to each of us who trek after his footprints today.

How This Book Is Organized

Portable Faith is organized into two parts. The first part, chapters 1–4, presents the *why*. It aspires to draw church attenders beyond the familiar, out of buildings and stages and classrooms, and into a wholly different definition of church. It presents church not as something you go to but as a way of living and being in your community.

This section is formatted in a series of insights—overarching principles, bits of wisdom, suggestions—that might be helpful as you create or renew your efforts to serve your surrounding community. These insights are woven together with pieces of my life story that often reference specific going-out activities I've helped design and lead. You may also want to visit my website, where there will be additional tips for how to carry out activities as an individual, group, or church. Although this content will likely be most relevant to people who lead a church, or who serve as volunteer leaders in one, my hope is it will prompt anyone seeking Jesus to a more portable expression of faith.

The second part, "Exercises for Portable Faith," is the very practical *how*. Here you will find a collection of hands-on exercises—developmental experiences, if you will—that might help recharge people's enthusiasm for the Great Commission and develop their sensitivity to their surrounding community. Anyone can participate in these experiences—individuals, small groups, college classes, or entire congregations. But if you're a church leader, you may choose to combine these exercises to create a reflective, nonlinear type of training designed to help people carry faith those first steps beyond your church building.

If there is any way I can support your college's or congregation's ambition to live and be church, please feel free to contact me. I enjoy speaking and consulting with congregations and denominational groups in person and also welcome readers to interact with me online via Twitter (@sarahcunning) or Facebook (www.facebook.com/ sarahcunninghampage).

The greatest good will be accomplished if we go to our world, not just as individuals or as single congregations, but as a generation of believers whose hearts collectively beat for those outside our church buildings. To encourage group conversation and invention, I invite you to share your responses and ideas with me and with others by visiting the "Portable Faith" tab at sarahcunningham.org.

Chapter One

The Origins of a Portable Faith

"The church?" The middle-aged woman behind the desk at the local bond office asked incredulously, tucking a stray strand of silvering-brown hair behind her ear. "I don't see how 'the church' would change anything about a community. There have been churches here since before the city was chartered."

The woman, although saying things that felt inflammatory to my seasoned religious ears, was difficult to dislike given her gentle-flowing tone and the weathered, mom-of-many smile lines that framed her eyes. I could imagine her bustling about a kitchen in a flour-covered apron, basting a turkey and offering me a tall glass of milk on Thanksgiving.

"There's at least a dozen churches within a four-block radius of here and that doesn't change anything." She gestured at the surrounding area almost sympathetically. "The city is the same as it's always been. Same problems, same hardship, same cycles. Churches hold weekly services for anyone who wants to come, but I don't think there's any reason to believe they impact people beyond their own buildings."

This was the comment, offered as nothing more than matter-of-fact observation, that set the course for the next five years of my life and influenced the way I would look at the world and faith for many years to come.

It was 1999.

I was a bold-to-a-fault, save-the-world twenty-something raised on a diet of communion and Sunday potlucks. And I was the *wrong* person . . . or maybe I was exactly the right person . . . to offer this comment to because it instantly and deeply offended me in a way that *changed my life.*

As I drove home from that day's round of interviews, which aimed to collect suggestions about how local churches could serve our city, tears stung the corners of my eyes. Not because I believed the woman's words to be purposefully assaulting or antagonistic, but for exactly the opposite reason. I could see on the woman's face, in her eyes, that she believed what she was saying in the deepest places of her being.

She assessed the church to be empty and void . . . *dead.*

And she was okay, even disturbingly at peace, with that.

But I was not.

The muscle-less, impact-less church secluded behind four brick walls this woman depicted was not the church I knew. It was not the community of believers envisioned by the Jesus I knew, or the one championed by the first-century followers of God I read about, either.

The most infuriating thing about the woman's commentary was that it was not wholly without merit.

Certainly, the faith community impacted our city in ways she didn't observe. I knew this for a fact. I'd seen the hearts of some churches melt for our community.

But it wasn't a mystery how the woman came to this conclusion. Most churches in our community had adopted a model that seemed, at least from outside appearance, to be based on "coming"—coming to Sunday services, Wednesday night services, small groups, vacation Bible schools, even softball games. And that meant the city residents most likely to be directly impacted by these churches were the people inside the church buildings.

Here is the church. Here is the steeple. Open up and see all the people.

Despite the popular children's rhyme and despite growing up as a pastor's kid and logging hundreds—maybe thousands—of hours in church pews, I knew in the sinking, what-is-true part of my gut that "coming" was not the verb Jesus had used in his parting shot to the disciples. "Come join us" was a decidedly different invitation than "go into all the world." And "inviting ones" was almost the polar opposite identity as "sent ones," the term attached to those first believing "apostles" who bore the message of Jesus.

The more I thought about the verbiage we lived out as churches, the more intensely I squinted at one of the core values of my own local church, which proclaimed "All People Matter to God."

All people. Inside the church, outside the church. People like the majority, people unlike the majority. All of them.

I was sure in my soul this was right. That all people mattered to God. Though I wasn't sure churches always knew exactly how to demonstrate how much we, and our God, valued the residents of our communities.

In my own small city, estimates claimed one out of six people were "churched." That meant about 16 percent of residents were thought to have a regular connection to a local Christian congregation. Churches, of course, knew how to demonstrate *this* 16 percent mattered. We spent all week crafting sermon series, designing graphics, churning out bulletins, creating children's programming, and hosting events for the one out of six people who would be *inside our buildings* each week.

But was this 16 percent supposed to be the only or even main group we intentionally built relationship with? And what was the best way to divide our focus between the one out of six people who showed up on Sundays wanting to know Jesus and the five-sixths of our local "world" whom we were specifically told to "go" and reach?

3

This of course is part of the timeless challenge the church or any institution faces. How do you rotate multiple priorities—church *and* community, coming *and* going, infrastructure *and* vitality—around the burners with enough regularity to keep every pan warm? Nevertheless, this challenge of learning to practice a more portable faith, individually and as a church, gripped me.

As I drove home from the day of interviews, I determined in the way messily passionate twenty-somethings do, that this goal of *going* to the "all" in "all people" would be one I would stake my life in. Thus, I set out to imagine new models. To figure out what it meant for me to live and be church in our community, first alongside the local church where I worked, and eventually by getting the chance to speak into many congregations beyond it.

As my determination to serve our surrounding community grew, my lead pastor and the board of elders invited me to develop our church's first-ever full-time staff position designed to build relationships with people outside our building's four walls.

This job was a blatant gift—perhaps one of the most important and generous of my life—and an ideal proving ground to test my hypotheses about living and being church. It provided a steady laboratory for learning how to practice faith again as a going community. That is not to say it was easy to inspire cultural and priority shifts in an already established church. Some days it wasn't. But in the everyday gains and setbacks attached to this new role, I developed a striking sense of confidence that the challenge of going to society's margins was not one that would or should be localized to only our church or our community.

And so, as our church forayed into new territory on the home front, I quietly began writing articles about "finding the all in all people" for denominational magazines. The content, I quickly found, seemed just as relevant and just as needed in Presbyterian materials or Evangelical Free ones as it was to my local nondenominational community.

As a result, over time, while interacting with other churches and denominations, while making plenty of mistakes and benefiting

4

from lots of gracious counsel, my fellow attenders and I learned a few things about how to live and be church and how to invite other like-minded believers to do the same.

The following pages contain the practical how-tos of how we learned to embed seeds in our church's programming that, over time, grew a more portable definition of faith. I've told pieces of this story before, wedged into the larger narratives of my first two books, *Dear Church: Letters From a Disillusioned Generation* and *Picking Dandelions: A Search for Eden Among Life's Weeds*, but most of this book is unshared content I was inspired to make available by audiences I've interacted with since 2006, when the first edition of *Dear Church* came out.

While traveling and speaking about my books, it didn't take me long to start wondering whether I'd written the wrong titles. After sweeping into a town and passionately delivering my thirty-minute spiel about why it was not okay that my generation was searching for truth everywhere but the one place Jesus appointed to dispense it, I would often allow time for a Q & A.

And this is the type of question that would arise. Almost every time:

"In the middle of the book, you mention that you offered single-parent car clinics. How did that work?"

My first answer was almost always philosophical, like the books. "We identified single parents as a group of people who sometimes felt marginalized by the church," I would say sweetly. "We then set out to value them by hearing their needs and caring for them."

The questioner would nod patiently, waiting for me to finish. "But what I want to know is *how* you did it. I mean, did you put up posters? How did you find the single parents? Who performed the work? Did the church underwrite any expenses?"

It was then I would often stare dumbfounded at the questioner, who now sat with a pen poised on top of a piece of paper, ready to write down my verbal instructions.

And I would realize maybe it would've been more practical to write a book that not only told the story of *why* I wanted to learn to *live and be* church outside the building's four walls but a book that also suggested a few ways for *how* others might do it as well.

Here, my friends, is the book and corresponding web resources I perhaps should've written in the first place.

Reflections on the Meaning of Church

For those of us who grew up over a lifetime of Sundays, weekend services were often seen as the happy climax to the church's spiritual week.

This was especially true in my case.

Sundays were noticeably elevated from the rest of my week. They were mysterious, sensuous, full of ambience. The wooden pews, whose ends curled into elegant swirls of carved wood, smelled faintly of Murphy's oil soap as they cushioned me in deep teal fabric. I felt enthroned on them. Poised for something important.

My foot would rock methodically as live music swelled to fill the sanctuary, sending drumbeats and vocal riffs floating to the glossy knotted pine rafters. My fingers traced the goose-bumped cover and translucent, tissue-thin pages of ancient Scripture. The rows of black and sometimes red print held story and wisdom worthy of its gold-rimmed pages. Even to a child, the reading was hearty and satisfying. An indulgence as sweet as chocolate and as filling as a Sunday roast.

By some great feat of architecture, even the church building itself seemed enchanted, as if positioned to pull in the high noon sun. And so just before the invitational hymn drew the audience to their feet, loose streams of sun would pierce the colored windows, painting a kaleidoscope of reflections onto the floor and walls.

The carpeted aisles people solemnly walked during altar calls were also known to hum with a sort of electric, person-to-person warmth as well. This collective charm was robust and nourishing, the type that resulted only when you gathered a familiar community from vantage points around the city to some pew or foyer or other holy meeting ground.

And in some rare moments, I remember, the room fell into a beautiful silence, as if some faint and sacred voice was whispering to everyone in attendance, entreating us to listen carefully. Taking us gently by the chins and lulling our minds into reflection and solitude.

It was a holy shushing.

At first, then, my definition of church was firmly rooted in childhood Sundays. So much so that it was difficult to imagine how a congregation might express faith outside of weekend service grandiose.

Initially, my ideas were thick with systems.

I focused on building formal partnerships between a lumbering religious institution and other organizations in the community. To benefit these local organizations, we started programs. And most of the programs—if I am honest—barely differed from our in-house teams and ministries. Attenders did little more than exchange the one or two hours they'd previously spent in small groups or Bible studies for one or two hours of equivalent time at a soup kitchen or public park.

It was a shallow trade-off that did little more than move our chess pieces from one place to another.

These ministry attempts didn't foster long-term relationships between people in our church and people outside of it. And they only filled small, designated windows of time during other days of the week, rather than inspiring a 24/7 lifestyle of being and living church.

In hindsight, the shortcomings of these initial attempts should not have been surprising. Getting at people's "insides" is an altogether bigger, more profound, and harder-to-measure undertaking than plugging them into mission trips or service projects. It is easy enough to slip attenders a schedule for preparing meals for the homeless every other Saturday from 2:00 to 4:00. It is much harder to inspire living, breathing humans to carry faith in their everyday breath and movements, everywhere they go.

Thankfully, though, our church continued learning and refining (not to mention making more mistakes) and eventually discovered more transforming ways of relating to our community.

The pages to come, then, are not designed to serve as a how-to manual, but to provide food for thought as you search for how to best live and be church in your community. As you read, I hope you will find principles to borrow from, build on, or take to a new level. But please take only what is useful and discard all that doesn't fit well in your context.

The ideas in this book are designed to be compatible with conventional church; to work alongside tradition without diminishing it or trying to show it up.

Church buildings are respected as important refuges of worship and learning, as sacred fixtures of community that preserve truths and ideals across geography and time. They house gatherings of people who—like the apostle Peter—know Jesus as the Christ, the son of the living God.

At the same time, the coming pages acknowledge faith existed in the deserts of Israel even before the Tabernacle or Temple were constructed. And that similarly, in Jesus' day, he didn't find the strongest belief in the synagogues, but on the margins of the New Testament world, in both people and places where it wasn't expected to surface.

This book suggests that faith, while often celebrated in churches, can still retain its portable qualities today. That it can rise in the warm, ambient lighting of a woodworked sanctuary but can just as validly seep through brick and mortar to grow up between people on a hillside or city street. That we can carry it wherever we go.

What you're about to read, then, doesn't seek to dismantle what you call church but rather to inspire wonder around how the ancient notion of *going* might deepen the way you live out your faith in God.

The phrase "church outreach" has been purposefully omitted from this book's title because the terms used by those in full-time ministry are too often dismissed by mainstream church attenders. Books labeled "outreach" too often only find homes on the shelves of church staff members who oversee outreach or evangelism programs. Or are only read by those perceived as "radicals," people who lead protests, lobby politicians, and leave the suburbs to live in the inner city.

But I firmly believe that when we treat the practice of the Great Commission like an assignment that belongs only to church staffs and social zealots, we do the rest of the people who follow Jesus a massive disservice. That we may, in fact, cheat ourselves out of the broader communal life God intended for us.

Portable Faith speaks to the development of belief itself, of how a person—*any person, anywhere*—wears faith in the normal routines of his or her life. It's an invitation for people of faith—social workers, soccer moms, capitol protestors, cubicle dwellers, activists, suburban home owners, white-collar workers, blue-collar workers, *everyone*— to imagine new ways of living and being church together.

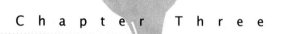

Insights on Being the Portable Church

Alas, we were not around in the first century to foot the hillsides with the disciples, arguing over whether it was polite to shoo away the children loitering around Jesus or whether it was reasonable to boot the hungry crowd to the nearest village to find their own bread.

Nor were we present for the holy hoopla of the early church, for the flaming tongues of fire, or for the fine dining and loot-sharing of Acts 2.

We don't know firsthand what the church looked, felt, or smelled like during the persecutions of Rome, the endorsement of Constantine, or the introduction of monastic communities. We didn't personally experience how it changed during the Great Schism, the Reformation, or the heyday of Puritanism. And we narrowly missed, by a couple hundred years, the circuit preachers and traveling revivalists of the Great Awakening and Second Great Awakening.

Somewhere in the twentieth or twenty-first centuries, the ecumenicals, fundamentalists, and charismatics broke onto the religious landscape, and in the long course of their rise to prominence, our generation and its church models were born.

We do, of course, know a few things about how we arrived at today's Western church models, mostly thanks to scraps of history passed through textbooks and church records.

We know, for example, that churches didn't meet in homes until designated spaces for worship became legal and even privileged under Constantine. That it wasn't until the eleventh century that a wave of cathedrals and parish churches started to surface across Western Europe. And that in the sixteenth century, the Catholics developed a taste for ornate churches with marble sculptures and gold fittings while the Protestants exchanged ancient altars for communion tables and pulpits.

But beyond that, we couldn't speak to the ins and outs of each period, and we wouldn't be wise to claim to know with any certainty what God thought of all of it. We can't be sure which parts of which era best expressed God's intentions, though we gather that things have changed drastically. If Peter and the rest of the disciples walked into a sixty-minute service with a live worship band and videos projected on the big screen and someone on the Hospitality Team shoved coffee cups into their hands, we wouldn't expect them to exclaim, "This is exactly like the gatherings of believers in our day!"

Our current notion of church passed through a couple thousand years, several thousand miles, countless evolutions, and plenty of hands by the time it arrived on our generation's doorstep. That means our identity has been being shaped for twenty centuries! Respecting our past, this book shares ideas that build on the church's ancient and recent history.

Because of this, some will find flaws with the ideas presented in this book simply because I attach them to existing church models. They will say the church is too mechanized or too influenced by imperialism and capitalism, that it still retains the weaknesses and sins of our modern, Westernized culture. They would rather declare the institution broken and start over. To get rid of the church buildings—to lighten our weight, so to speak—in our efforts to go to the world.

I get where they're coming from. My first book, *Dear Church:*

Letters from a Disillusioned Generation, expressed some dissatisfaction with current church methods and models too. Like others, if I were waking to the blank canvas of the first century, I too might entertain different ideas for how to carry out the Great Commission than the steepled buildings or once-a-week services that come to mind when the word "church" is spoken in the West. But the reality is that our generation's canvas isn't blank, it's already occupied by a globe of churches and two millennia worth of religious practices.

I cannot, in good conscience, suggest we divorce ourselves from that identity—from millions who pray to our Creator, from the best findings of our forebearers, or from the heroes of faith—the Peters, the Pauls, the Ignatiuses, the Luthers, the Moodys—who forged our path.

For all its flaws, I cannot responsibly advocate abandoning the church's journey.

It has too much strength in its bones.

Too many resources in its pews.

Too much wisdom in its history.

Not to mention, far too many church people are trying to do good in the name of Jesus, and this is what Jesus said shows us they are with us and not against us.

Rather than detach from a planet full of churches and from the collective wisdom of previous generations of believers, then, *Portable Faith* starts with now. It is designed to build on today's church models, even if they are sometimes imperfect models forged and maintained by imperfect people who routinely fail to capture God's full intentions for human life.

I don't think today's church is a terrible place to start because it requires us, like generations before us, to wrestle with God for ourselves. To decide if we, like Jacob, are just mindlessly trudging along after Abraham or whether we will welcome him to renew his covenant in new ways in our generation.

It gives us the chance, through refining our church models, to declare that God is our God and we too are God's people.

And it trusts that in humankind's journey of redemption with God, God always seems to let us start where we are, however flawed and dysfunctional that might be.

#1 We Are Motivated by Frustration

Sometimes the people most drawn to a more portable faith are the ones who are most disillusioned with current church models. Religious infrastructure has let them down along the way. And although they may still attend weekend services, they're dying to reimagine the way church and faith typically happen.

Clearly, the opinions of frustrated people are not always helpful, but if we are willing to look, they often—sometimes even unintentionally—point to possibility. At the root of many complaints is a desire for change, a yearning for a new way of being and living faith. Tension between the way things are and the way things could be is an important source of ideas for the future church.

So frustrations will always be voiced.

I'm so sick of this church. There's got to be another way for churches to relate to people that is more real, more organic, or more (fill in the blank).

You know what I say?

Good! Be sick. Be disgusted. Be dissatisfied.

It's often only when we become nauseated with the way things are that we can develop a vision for what can be. It's only when the fit gets tight and restricting that we tweak or discard our model for one that fits our church bodies. It's only when we are on the verge of insanity, when we're exhausted or wounded to tears with religion, that we find incentive to seek better ways to live and be church.

Maybe it is then and only then that some of us can really *go*.

Without the dissatisfaction, we might be resistant to moving.

We might be suspicious of attempts to get outside our buildings. We might be tightly clutching a model that has attached the wrong verb to the Great Commission.

We might be like the president of a bank who spends all his time polishing the tube that delivers money to drive-through customers but routinely leaves the safe unlocked with the door ajar. We might be protecting the church model, the chute that delivers our item of value, rather than the valuables themselves.

Probing our frustrations with existing models may help us unclench our fingers from around the way we've always done things. And in doing so, we may find what is really valuable, allowing all the excess systems and programs that our churches don't need to drop from our hands.

Sometimes our frustrations underline selfishness, control issues, or other sins that have slowly and perhaps unintentionally crept into the way we organize church. Digging into these tensions can be painful and volatile, but it can lead us back to humility, to renewing our place as lifelong learners at the feet of Jesus. When we return to Jesus as our center point, the need to fight and protect our models often dies. And maybe, just maybe, something new—something more suited for going, something more portable—will be birthed in its place.

One of the most accidentally effective things I ever did when I was trying to imagine a more portable faith was to use my first appearance on our church's stage to press into my frustration. Although I'd given plenty of welcome speeches and announcements in the past, that was the first time I was invited to share in the actual speaking time. I nervously climbed the steps, perched on top of a stool in the center spotlight, and issued an invitation. Perhaps the only invitation a fumbling, disillusioned idealist like me could issue. An invitation to get frustrated.

In college I had visited and studied in urban settings around the country—most notably, spending two semesters in a homeless shelter in Chicago. Many of these experiences fueled my frustrations with church efforts. I found my vision in this tension with organized

religion, which was captured in the stories of many inspiring people
I met along the way.

With her permission, I invited our church attenders into the
story of Lisa, whose story illustrated her frustrations and underlined
many of mine. Lisa had grown up in a single-parent family with a
mother who had, as Lisa called it, a "thing" for alcohol. Her mother
also dabbled in cocaine and dated a man who delivered unmarked
"packages," which Lisa later learned belonged to a local drug dealer.
Lisa's mom had always struggled to cover their household bills, and
she'd always seemed fatigued by the demands of being a single parent,
but the more she became involved with this particular boyfriend, the
more unstable the household became. While Lisa was still in early
elementary school, for example, her mother began leaving the girl at
home alone.

"At first, it was just for a few minutes. Maybe fifteen," Lisa
explained. On these occasions, Lisa's mom instructed the girl to stay in
her bedroom while she made a quick run to the store to pick up milk or
to fill up her gas tank before hurrying home. Over time, however, Lisa's
mom stayed away longer periods, often stretching late into the night.

Eventually, Lisa's mom and her mom's boyfriend found a new
place to confine the little girl when they left her home alone: a
second-story deck that overlooked the backyard. The deck was a six-
by-six platform enclosed by a railing, with no steps leading up or
down.

Most times Lisa was locked on the deck were brief, yet there
were times when her mom spent hours away from home. Lisa
recounted to me how at least once it rained, leaving her exposed to
the elements without an umbrella or any source of covering. In those
moments, Lisa pulled her shirt up over her head like a makeshift hood
and huddled against the house's siding. Another time, when her
bladder could wait no longer, she was forced to urinate through the
floorboards.

Lisa's only source of support or relief, in those stretches, was
her neighbor Katie, who was a year younger than Lisa. Katie, an
outgoing elementary school student who wore her hair in pigtails,

sometimes sat and talked to Lisa over the fence that separated their backyards. "She was the only person who ever helped me. She even threw me snacks when I was stuck out there at mealtimes," Lisa said.

On one particular day, Lisa's mom was gone for a longer-than-usual stretch, and as a result, Lisa missed both lunch and dinner. Fortunately, after Lisa had been stranded for hours on the deck, Katie emerged. "As soon as I told her how hungry I was, she went and made a sandwich. She put it in a Ziploc bag and tried to throw it up to me."

Unfortunately, Katie was still young and a bit uncoordinated, and her aim was not accurate. Lisa watched with disappointment as the sandwich landed with a thud on the shingles of the roof right above and to the left of the deck where Lisa sat. It was completely out of her hungry reach.

"I tried to keep my mind off it," Lisa told me. "I tried not to look up. I sang little songs to myself to distract from my hunger, but eventually, I just cracked."

After a couple more hours, Lisa decided her only hope was to climb up on the roof to recover the food. "I got up on the railing somehow and was holding onto the gutter above me to keep steady. Then I put my foot on the porch light and tried to pull myself onto the roof. I managed to wiggle myself about halfway up, but I was cold and tired, and I just didn't have the strength to keep going. My arms started shaking, my teeth started chattering. And then I fell."

Lisa's hands clutched at the shingles and the gutter in an attempt to hang on, but she was unable to recover her grip. She plummeted to the ground while screaming. "And then I just kept screaming," she remembered, "because as I tried to break my fall, my arm got jammed into the ground. But even as I lay there, I was more worried about my mom coming home and punishing me for leaving the deck than I was about my arm."

Lisa's arm was broken—fractured in several places—something she wouldn't have known if it weren't for the EMTs that Katie's grandmother called to the scene.

After Lisa explained to the paramedics how she had gotten hurt, and she was taken to the hospital where the staff asked her more follow-up questions, Lisa's case was reported to Child Protective Services. When she was released from the hospital the next day, she was assigned to the first of several foster homes.

Lisa eventually escaped a neglectful home, but she was never able to escape the stigma that came along with it. Because she still lived in the same community, many people—even in her new life—knew her mom or at least knew of her mom's reputation. Some had such disgust for her mom's lifestyle that when one of Lisa's foster mothers took her to church, several parents told their kids to avoid Lisa. At least one even prohibited her child from going to Sunday school with her. They feared, out of misplaced concern, that Lisa—like her mother—would be a bad influence on their kids. The girl who spent much of life locked outside on a deck alone now felt as though she'd been locked out of church as well.

After finishing Lisa's story, I knew most people in our congregation probably assumed the incident occurred in Chicago or Detroit or one of the other larger urban areas where I'd done work.

"But this didn't happen in some poverty-stricken neighborhood in one of our country's largest metropolitan areas." I was quick to clarify in closing, "Lisa is a girl about my age, who grew up here in this town, less than three miles from this church building. That means the church parents who worried about Lisa's background weren't wealthy elitists in some posh Chicago financial district. They were everyday, working-class members of our city. And the context where Lisa learned as a child that churches didn't have a place for people like her? That was the community where you and I still live today.

"Lisa lives and works in our city every day, still unsure of whether any local congregations will ever be willing to make a place for her."

As I finished telling Lisa's story, it was as if I'd shown them a mural—like the ones that graffiti artists create about injustice—spray-painted onto the air of the sanctuary. The auditorium was eerily quiet, the congregation lost in the silence that springs not from boredom but from thoughtful and perhaps surprised reflection.

I sincerely didn't know whether the congregation was following along with me, or if they were offended by what I said. But I went on.

"I don't know about you, but I'm frustrated by Lisa's story. I'm dissatisfied not only that people like Lisa might've had such an experience here in our community. But I'm heartbroken that in some people's deepest moments of need, those who follow Christ might have chosen to be purposefully distant."

Mustering all the hope I had for that moment, I asked the congregation to join me in being dissatisfied with the outcome of Lisa's life.

To get dissatisfied with the face of the church Lisa experienced. To get upset by the woman mentioned in the first chapter of this book, who believed the church had made no impact on the community where we lived. To get annoyed that residents searching for truth and hope sometimes felt abandoned by the community Jesus commissioned to carry them.

As the congregation left the church building that day, I asked them to take that dissatisfaction with them. The benediction was "May God bless you, may his face shine upon you, and may you be dissatisfied."

And by God's mysterious grace, dissatisfaction spread, as dissatisfaction almost always does (for good or bad). That Sunday, we closed the service by passing out response cards at the end of the service. Nearly two hundred people signed up to help in the ministry efforts to our community that day. And a local insurance salesman, whose heart had been moved by the story, offered to donate five thousand dollars to our work, even though I hadn't asked for a penny.

That day, the topic—frustration—was one that sprang naturally from my personal angst rather than stemming from an understanding about how to give a persuasive speech. But I unintentionally learned something important about the power of frustration that day: it doesn't have to be feared. It often propels people into new vision.

Frustration may be just the fuel needed to get a church going.

> **Summary: Do not fear your frustration, dissatisfaction, and disillusionment. Use these reactions as motivation to reflect and act.**

#2 We Remember Where God Is

As a child, I was always fascinated by the Old Testament story about the prophet Elijah visiting one of Israel's impoverished widows. She was struggling to meet the needs of her small family, and he, in return, did one of the most practical and tangible miracles of the Bible. He prayed for God to multiply the woman's oil so she could resell it.

I loved that Elijah brought God to the woman not by reading orally from a scroll but by embodying God's care for her and doing something practical to respond to her need. His stop by the woman's house left her better off than when he arrived.

As a child, I had no idea that the tenth chapter of Luke existed, but when I discovered it later in life, I was similarly smitten. It's the passage where Jesus sends out his seventy-two followers to homes in the community.

"When you enter a house, first say, 'Peace to this house,'" Jesus instructed his followers. "If someone who promotes peace is there, your peace will rest on them; if not, it will return to you" (Luke 10:5-6).

Peace, the gift of those who *went*, I later learned implied a sense of security, safety, prosperity, and spiritual contentedness. The fact that Jesus indicated his followers could carry that sort of peace with them inspired me that perhaps we, too, could transport God's goodness in our beings, in our words, or by our presence. To present the blessing he would give if he were where we are.

There was something romantic and noble about this revelation. We, the servants of a compassionate King, can then walk the streets on his behalf. We can greet villagers, shake hands, and kiss babies as if the King has asked us to be his ambassadors, to communicate his desire for the people's well-being.

Because he *has*.

As we interact in the public sphere, we convey the heart of the empire. In these moments, we live and breathe the faith of Elijah and the seventy-two and many more after them. Belief can be portable! It has legs, wheels, wings!

And yet the flip side of that is as we bring faith with us into the community dozens of generations later, it's wise to remember we are probably not the first to carry Jesus to our region. God's fingerprints have likely been left all over our area, bearing witness to how many times God touched it over the years.

He is likely already present in our community.

This fact was underlined to me as I read a book about the city in which I live. The book contained records and information about the early days of our city before Michigan was even a territory. As I was flipping through it one day, I came across a story about a handful of young settlers who journeyed miles on foot to be baptized *prior to the formation of the city*, before the territory was even recognized as the State of Michigan.

Long before my time, my parents' time, and even my grandparents' time, before our city or state was listed on a map, people were practicing their faith in the fields and dirt paths of our community.

From then on, I had a more humble awareness that neither I nor our church was responsible for God's introduction to our community. If anything, we were the ones now being introduced into the story God had been unfolding in our community for generations.

Because of this, as churches attempt to go to their communities, it might be wise for us to look for the places where God is already present. To build on the foundations laid by followers of God who went before us. Rather than assume our church must start ministries or programs that address the needs of our communities, we might seek to understand the people and organizations that have already been bringing God's intentions to their communities and join them.

There is practical value to joining others too. For example, it allows us to tap into existing wisdom, to learn from the experiences of those who walked the community's streets before us. Also, pragmatically speaking, joining an existing effort is often less expensive because the initial start-up costs and energy investment have already been made. Not to mention, we may bring fresh enthusiasm and energy to a team of people or organization badly in need of reinforcements.

The idea of coming alongside existing ministries and organizations can be a difficult sell in some church contexts because often churches are used to staffing and funding only their own enterprises. For example, they send checks to their denomination's missionaries, or they invest money in their ministries and programs, which they control completely.

I remember the first time we were able to shift a small amount of our church's money into the hands of those outside our church who were ministering in the community. Probably less than one hundred dollars changed hands, but its release was an important indicator of the paradigm shift our church was undergoing.

In this first case, a woman in the church knew of someone who worked in the local prison and needed Bibles to give to inmates in a group she was leading. Neither the person doing the ministering nor the inmates ever attended our church. Nevertheless, we funded the purchase of Bibles because it aligned with our aim to support what God was already doing in the community.

The effort was reminiscent of an old country church with no budget, no fiscal board, and no policies. When they heard about a need for something like Bibles, there was no procedural book to consult; they—the gathering of people—tried to meet the need, or they didn't. Whether they rallied depended not on their ability to get through budgetary red tape but on their ability to humanize the people whose needs were presented to them and on their ability to respond to God's promptings.

Partnering with other people and organizations in the community is often an expression of humility—a reminder that although we bear God to our world, we are not the sole source of God's light. Accepting this truth helps us stay healthier in our service. We may not be as likely to burn ourselves out because we recognize that even if we take a break, God's handiwork in the community goes on. Also, when we honor other people's efforts, we may help guard our hearts against pride that assumes we are the only ones vested with legitimate vision for our communities.

> **Summary: We are likely not the first to bear God to a community; God is likely already there.**

#3 We All Sign On

Many times, when a church begins to set foot in the surrounding community, when it first strikes out to build relationships with people on society's margins, a small group of passionate people lead the charge. Maybe the lead visionary is a man who just returned home from a mission trip or a woman with a background in social work. Or maybe an attender or two just had a run-in with a local person in need, which spurred them to champion the church's interactions outside its building.

Only a few people are needed to start things. So it's a positive to have even one person, let alone a handful, catch a vision for building relationships in the community. It's similarly good when these people form outreach ministries or when they attempt as a group to pool attender resources to meet community needs, such as raising money for a family whose house burned down or recruiting people to go on an overseas mission trip.

But if the church is going to maintain a *going* posture, it's important—even crucial—to involve the rest of the congregation as soon as possible.

As in any organization or company, the more insiders who embrace the value of building relationships with the community, the more that value will become part of the group's identity. It's the difference between being a church where *some people sometimes go* and being a *going* church.

If a couple of doctors in a hospital, for example, decide to champion the value of timeliness and try to cut patients' waiting room time in half, the experience of many patients will improve. But it might also create confusion or bad impressions when one person's doctor sees her after five minutes of waiting and another person has to wait an hour. Even among the doctors, it could potentially create feelings of competition, with one group perceiving the other is trying to show them up.

But if the majority of doctors take up this goal to reduce patient waiting time, it is no longer a pet movement of a small group. It becomes part of the hospital's identity in the community. The hospital gains a reputation as an efficient organization that—as a whole—values putting people first. And the impact is intensely multiplied. Almost every patient benefits from hospital-wide improvements.

Along the same lines, in a church, it is best when not just one person is passionate about outreach but an entire group of people commit to valuing and getting to know the surrounding community.

When this happens, congregation members are on the same page, inviting all of them to learn and reflect on how the church approaches the Great Commission. Church-wide ownership of the value helps prevent one group from feeling uncomfortable or unaware of what another is doing. And it also builds a more cohesive gathering for community members to visit, lowering the risk that a person could be invited by a friendly, intentional member of the outreach team only to then be ignored or, worse yet, sense tension from other members.

Although every attender is not going to invest in the community at the same level, every single person in the church can be part of the journey.

Here are some ways to involve the entire congregation:

Get as many people as you can to go through reflective, experiential exercises like the ones found at the end of this book. To do this, it may be helpful to offer the experiences at convenient, varied times on different days of the week, so attenders can find a time to participate regardless of their work shifts or children's extracurricular schedules. You'll also likely have the best participation if you make these meetings as convenient as possible, offering food for those who come straight from work or child care for those who can't find a babysitter. In addition, it may be best to offer these developmental experiences in several formats. One group might meet every Monday lunch hour for two months; another might do two all-day Saturday trainings; another might hold a weekend retreat that offers a fast-track version of the material.

It doesn't matter whether one group does less of the exercises or gets through less information than another group. What matters is that the majority of attenders are encouraged to think about how faith and faith practices can be carried outside the church building.

The downside of doing multiple trainings is that not everyone will be able to come, so some people—whatever percentage are not persuaded or able to attend—may continue to operate in the dark about the church's new or growing initiative in the community.

Arrange for the trainings to come to them. Instead of having to recruit attenders, set up rooms, and present these experiences multiple times, you might opt to take the material and exercises to places where the people already are. For example, you could work with the pastor or teaching team to design a sermon series around these ideas and then try to integrate some of the experiences into usual weekend services.

A number of exercises in this book can be completed in the church auditorium without going anywhere. An alternative to doing the exercises together, however, would be to have the pastor challenge attenders to complete one experience on their own in their free time, using instructions printed in the church bulletin.

If you opt to challenge church attenders to complete exercises at home during the week, posting reminders on Facebook, Twitter, the church website, or in e-mail newsletters throughout the week may be helpful. You may even ask social network friends and followers to post their stories about their weekly challenges on your church's site or Facebook page. Each story will not only remind others to do their challenges but will also reinforce going as a shared value of the church.

Again, not every person will complete the activities, but even if only 10 percent do, you may be able to select a few members to share about their experiences from stage the next week or even to share videos of people engaging some of the community exercises. By sharing the experiences of a few, the church further underlines that going is an important value of the whole congregation, which will further encourage other attenders to take on the next challenges.

If you try this option, you may also consider inviting absent attenders or people who begin attending at a later date to go back and complete the challenges. Being able to access the recordings of the message the pastor shared the day the challenge was issued will further orient them to the church's emphasis on going.

Another way of distributing information and raising awareness about new initiatives would be to do some community exercises with the church's small-group leaders and ask them to repeat the exercises with their group members. Although small groups still won't be able to distribute the information to every single attender, they will likely get the material to the core group of most involved attenders.

Set aside time to do ministry as a group or a church. Choose an event in your city or region where large numbers of people could serve or work together. Or set aside a Sunday morning to go out and do a service project or other experience together. Want to do something really spontaneous? Stage an Ambush Sunday or Destination Sunday.

Ambush Sunday/Destination Sunday

Three weeks prior to the date appointed as "Ambush" or "Destination Sunday," begin forewarning attenders that on this designated day, church will be held at a surprise, to-be-announced location. Make it clear that "church" will take place elsewhere in the city, but keep the events of the day a surprise, except for providing basic information such as what type of clothing will be appropriate to wear and how long you expect the event to take. Depending on the activity you end up scheduling for the day, you may also want to ask attenders to bring task-specific materials (writing utensils, shovels, rakes, paintbrushes, cleaning products, and so forth).

In the time leading up to the special day, it will be helpful to post repeated reminders in the church bulletin, website, community e-mails, or social networks to prepare people for the upcoming day. During on-stage announcements, it may also be wise to have the speaker stress that everyone is encouraged to come to Destination Sunday, as it is not a special event for just a few people, but an alternative site for regular church.

Choose a site that can accommodate a large group of people. Although it is unlikely your whole congregation will participate, it is possible that you will draw a large crowd of attenders who've become curious about what the church is doing. Possible meeting places include fairgrounds, playgrounds, parks, walking trails, nature preserves, and school campuses. Then, choose an activity to do together. The easiest tasks for such a large group might be cleaning up a community space, painting over graffiti, repainting and repairing a playground, or picking up litter alongside roads in commercial areas. A smaller congregation might want to do deep cleaning, repair work, painting, or donation sorting for a local nonprofit, nursing home, or shut-in. A larger congregation, however, might need to divide up the group into several small teams, disperse teams to several different projects, and get back together afterward.

Don't feel as though the Destination Sunday has to involve a service project, however. You could choose to have attenders walk around the city or a certain public space and ask them to spend time in reflection and prayer for the community. You could break them into small groups and provide discussion questions. You could take them to a site that overlooks the city and have the pastor preach a Jesus-inspired hillside sermon about the church's vision for living faith in your community.

When the designated day arrives, you'll want to post greeters and/or signs at all the church's main entrances to direct any uninformed attenders to the mystery site. Depending on the task at hand, it might also be helpful to offer nursery or child care at the church building. There is value in designing certain Destination Sundays to be family affairs that allow children to participate alongside their parents. But for projects that are not kid-friendly, or are only appropriate for older children, offering nursery or children's ministry may be a determining factor in making it possible for adults to get involved. If you do offer children's programming, consider doing something with the children that allows them to make a positive contribution to the community. For example, they could clean up the church grounds outside or they could make cards to thank community servants such as police officers or firefighters.

Whatever you decide to do on a Destination Sunday, you may want to recruit a group of volunteers to serve as guides during the experience as well. These people would be appointed to make sure arriving attenders are ushered to the right place and to help make sure everyone is able to participate. In service tasks, this can be particularly important, as attenders may not always know how to take the initiative. They may need someone to come alongside them and suggest things for them to do. Guides could be drawn from outreach-oriented ministry teams—people who would be naturally interested in sharing their year-round heart for the community or they could be drawn from regular Sunday morning teams like ushers, greeters, or hospitality team members.

No matter what agenda you choose for a Destination Sunday, it can be helpful to provide some sort of guided processing time at its completion. You may decide to build this reflection time into the large group experience by appointing a few people to share their thoughts, you may decide to provide discussion points and have people break into pairs or small groups, or you may ask people to submit reflections and feedback via e-mail, the church website, Facebook, or another online platform. The feedback time should be focused on building awareness of how the day's activities are connected to biblical instruction, Jesus' example, and your church's mission. Feedback time might also be used to survey people about the level of comfort they felt engaging a new experience.

You may think it's unusual, but odds are, people will be intrigued enough not to want to miss a mysterious experience. The Ambush Sunday will be different enough from typical Sundays that it will become a memorable milestone in your congregation's history. People will remember and talk about it.

Start with just one Destination Sunday and observe, as it unfolds, what things you might improve upon the next time you attempt a similar event. Then, if it's feasible and you find it serves your church's aims, you may want to set up some sort of regular schedule, planning to do one Destination Sunday per quarter or even one per month. You could also choose to do a series of Destination Sundays, perhaps doing Destination Sundays for four or six weeks in a row during the summer.

If you do choose to incorporate them into your church's yearly schedule, keep in mind you do not have to sustain the same schedule for all eternity. If you kick off an emphasis on outreach by doing one Destination Sunday per month the first year, and you find this schedule burns out the people planning or executing these events, you can always cut back to doing them less frequently. Even doing Destination Sundays two or three times a year would go a long way toward getting the entire congregation to engage their minds in the value of going to the community.

If you'd like some help setting up and hosting your first Destination Sunday, or would like to invite me to speak at your event, feel free to e-mail me at sarahraymondcunningham@gmail.com.

Set up opportunities for every ministry area or small group to do a service project or to go on a mission trip together. Have one motivated person or a team of people take on the role of coordinating service projects for the church. These individuals will create a database of needs in the community and invite each small group to adopt an organization to help.

To begin, the coordinating volunteers should e-mail or phone local organizations that might be in need of service. This includes the city government, nonprofits, rec centers, and even schools or other churches. In their communication, coordinators can ask each community organization what sorts of needs it has, particularly what kinds of needs might be able to be resolved by a team of volunteers. While speaking to each organization, it will be helpful for the coordinating volunteers to record certain information, such as the name of the organization, the contact name of the employee they speak to, and details about the need that is mentioned. If the need requires specific materials, such as painting the facility, the coordinators should also ask if the organization can provide the paint, brushes, rollers, and drop cloths or whether they would need the painting supplies to be provided.

The information collected can then be entered into a spreadsheet or typed into a list to be shared with small-group leaders. Small-group leaders can then be asked to review the list of options, perhaps even sharing the list with their small group, and choose one listed need to meet. If a small-group leader chooses a need which requires the purchase of supplies, there are several options for getting the cost of these materials covered. One would be to allocate money in the church's budget to cover materials needed for service projects. Another option would be to challenge small-group members to donate the cost of the supplies or the supplies themselves. In addition, small-group members could contact local businesses and attempt to get some materials donated.

Before small groups go out to complete service projects, it can be helpful for leaders to do a brief, ten-minute orientation with the group. And after the project is completed, it can be helpful to do some sort of follow-up reflection.

During the orientation, the small-group leader might offer a reminder of how acts of service express the church's mission and demonstrate God's care for all people. They might also challenge participants to stretch themselves beyond their normal comfort zones, to try to be exceptionally generous and do more than what is asked of them, and to strive to keep peace even if they encounter some sort of tension with a bossy, angry, or otherwise offensive employee or client of the organization being served. Encourage participants to be prayerful and to see the experience as less about trying to "help the poor" and more about trying to align themselves with God's heart and obey his commands to serve those in need. Invite them to observe their own feelings and communicate their own misgivings and challenges along the way, in an attempt to focus their energy not only on the "recipients" but on their own personal development.

The feedback time should be focused on building awareness of how the day's activities are connected to biblical instruction, Jesus' example, and your church's mission. The leader might also survey people about the level of comfort they felt engaging a new experience.

If a small group has a particularly positive experience, encourage them to establish a long-term relationship with the organization served. Perhaps, for example, they could return to the organization on a regular or irregular schedule to lengthen their service and build more authentic relationships with the organization's staff and clients.

As with Destination Sundays, small-group service projects can be integrated into the church's yearly calendar as they fit. You may decide to challenge small groups to do a certain number of service projects a year or you may just keep them informed about community needs and allow each group to determine how many they'd like to take on. If coordinators accumulate enough community needs, the needs could even potentially prompt another Destination Sunday, where attenders could break into groups and complete the projects during the normal service time.

Again, a service project may not expose attenders to all the ideas you'd like to share or all the experiences you'd like them to have, but it may be a start. The point is to whet the appetite of as many people as possible, orient them to the church's new focus, and inspire them to feel ownership when they hear information shared about other community initiatives. At our church, even the kids' ministry was able to partner in some projects.

The more people who increase their openness to building relationships outside the church, the more your church as a whole will adopt a portable expression of faith.

An added bonus of having many people involved is that staffing smaller endeavors will be easier. When more than four hundred people had been through the training at the church where I worked, it was suddenly easy to find twenty-five people to take on a work project in urban Chicago.

Another bonus of having a large group of people involved is that there will be less burnout. It's not just three save-the-world types trying to rally everyone to do good. Building relationships in the surrounding community is an ambition everyone bears together.

One of the most powerful examples I've witnessed of an entire church aligning around the value of going occurred when Mark and Sheila, two attenders at the church where I worked, developed a vision for serving the children of inmates in our city.

This couple worked with a national organization to help meet the needs reported by the families of prisoners who lived in our community. Because our city housed the state prison, we had a disproportionate amount of need—enough that we worried our goal might be a bit too ambitious. But Mark and Sheila quickly went to work recruiting other attenders to purchase various items the families of our city's prisoners needed, and their faith paid off! Because our church attenders had such compassionate hearts and because, as a church, we'd already been emphasizing our intention of caring for our community, so many people responded to Mark and Sheila's initial pleas that the church was able to meet all the identified needs in our community the first week of our campaign.

At first, we saw this as the successful end to that specific effort. But when Mark and Sheila reported their success to the director of the organization we were working with, they discovered a sad reality. The director was pleased to hear about Mark and Sheila's success but lamented that our church's reaction was not always typical. "We have more than one hundred children with needs in the Detroit area who we've been unable to help," she confided.

The director was not at all trying to inspire Mark and Sheila to take responsibility for the unmet needs facing her organization. She was simply talking off the cuff about the ups and downs of their efforts. And because of that, Mark and Sheila could have clearly offered their sympathy and prayers and walked away untouched by this admission of need in the nearby city of Detroit. Instead, they were haunted by the idea of children who were already facing many challenges going without items they needed. As a result, Mark and Sheila brought this excess need from outside our community to the church and challenged the church to dig deeper. Not only did they ask the people to cover more than one hundred extra children who weren't even from our community, but they apologetically explained the challenge came with a new obstacle. "Because these children don't live in our community, we can't hand-deliver presents," they explained. "We have to raise the cost of shipping each present out of our city."

As this extra obligation was revealed to our congregation, I remember mentally calculating how much I had in my ministry budget and in my personal savings, fully expecting that there would be a shortage when attempting to cover the massive shipping costs. I knew that a growing group of maybe twenty people considered themselves to be especially passionate about outreach, and I secretly hoped this small group of zealous people might cooperate to help me cover the charges. I am confident this small group of movers and shakers would've risen to the occasion, but fortunately, I never had to find out because a much better scenario unfolded. By the end of the three weekend services, every remaining need listed for the city of Detroit had been met, and one couple in the church stepped forward to donate the money to ship all of the packages.

Every victory, though, seemed to present a new challenge. Packages that needed to be shipped also needed to be packed, for instance. Having so many items donated meant there was more work to be done than we had originally anticipated—far more work than the original ministry team who had assembled around the project could complete on their own. So once again Mark and Sheila went back to the congregation and invited anyone who was willing to bring wrapping paper, tape, and gift tags and gather in the church's lobby the next week to wrap the presents and pack them in boxes to be shipped.

Despite the congregation's generosity in purchasing items, Mark and Sheila and I were still uncertain about how involved the many educated professionals in our community would want to become in the more menial, behind-the-scenes tasks. I remember very clearly the mix of faith and fear that entered into our conversation on wrapping and delivery day as we waited to see whether anyone beyond our initial team would stay to help.

But I remember even more clearly what I saw when I stepped out of the auditorium after service: an army of people bearing wrapping and shipping supplies. With enthusiasm and precision, operating as if they shipped hundreds of presents on a daily basis, they spread out to all corners of the building, squatting, kneeling, and sitting on the floor, holding and turning and taping boxes. By the end of the day, every present had been wrapped, packed, and either hand-delivered or labeled for shipping. After seeing all of this unfold, I was even able to tag along to Mark's company, which allowed a small team of our volunteers to use its scales and shipping equipment to correctly attach adequate postage to each package. The endeavor was a complete success!

After a long and blessed day of watching our congregation respond to its surrounding communities, I returned to the church building to clean up. I found that every scrap of paper and wad of tape had been picked up and taken to the Dumpster by church attenders. I also found boxes bearing dozens of unopened rolls of donated wrapping paper, and a note that read, "We left these just in case any more items came in to be wrapped. If not, feel free to keep for future efforts."

As I slipped each roll of paper into storage, I couldn't help feeling a little bit like the disciples counting up the baskets of excess loaves and fish after the five thousand had been fed. I was well aware that we would not have been able to meet such a massive need had we been forced to rely on just the volunteers associated with outreach ministries. The impact we experienced that day results only when an entire faith community comes together around the same goal.

Summary: Invite the entire church to join in building relationships with your community. This is the only way to move from being a few attenders who go to becoming a going church.

#4 Our Leaders Buy In

Get your lead pastor behind you, or get out.

This is my suggestion to people who desire to lead their churches into their surrounding communities. But before these were my words, they were Wayne Gordon's.

I first encountered Wayne "Coach" Gordon in college while I was completing an internship with the Christian Community Development Association (CCDA). The CCDA, whose story is captured in the book *Real Hope in Chicago*, began with an inspiring group of people who came together to reclaim their Chicago community from poverty and violence. By buying up buildings in their neighborhood and reclaiming abandoned and crime-ridden property for the common good, the community started a church, a health clinic, a counseling center, an after-school program, a residential substance abuse facility, a gymnasium, apartment complexes, and more, all in the same city block!

The hope they nurtured in the community of Lawndale was so noticeable that people from outside the region even began moving to the area just to be a part of their work. As a result, when I visited

Lawndale's Sunday morning church service two decades after the work began, I observed attenders from an unusually wide range of ethnic and class backgrounds.

This atypical mix of attenders got my attention. So I met with Coach Gordon at CCDA headquarters with one pressing question on my mind. "You've been able to lower typical race and class barriers and bring diverse people together in the same congregation," I noted. "Do you think it's possible for a suburban white or middle-class church to do the same thing? Could churches in those kinds of settings lower the social walls and attract people of all races and classes as well?"

Coach Gordon nodded to indicate he'd heard the question, but there was a lengthy and obvious pause as he considered how he wanted to respond.

"You know what? I'm going to give you a very qualified yes," he finally replied.

Coach Gordon went on to caution me that a grassroots movement, where an attender tries to influence a congregation to adopt new values, would be nearly impossible. "Get your lead pastor behind you," he advised, "or get out." And then he smiled and added, "And come work with us."

When I returned home, I set out to follow Coach Gordon's advice and secure my pastor's support before trying to intentionally expand our church's relationships with diverse people groups.

It was harder than I expected.

My impassioned, bold-to-a-fault pleas sounded young and unfocused—like I was pitching a plan to pour soup down the throats of every homeless person rather than to advance the aim of our church to lead people to full life in Christ.

After months of doing research, sharing stories, citing statistics, drawing sketches—everything short of doing back-handsprings through his office—to keep my pastor's attention, our communication improved. And the pastor and I forged a lasting friendship. But although he became increasingly supportive of me as an individual, there was little to suggest he would endorse a full-fledged ministry along the lines I was proposing.

One day, however, I stumbled into an off-the-cuff conversation with my pastor that may have taken both of us by surprise. "I think I'm going to look for jobs in the nonprofit sector," I confessed. "They seem to be able to serve people on society's margins in a way most churches can't."

My pastor wasn't buying what I was selling.

"No, Sarah, you don't want to do that," he said in a tone that was more advisory than argumentative. "The church is the institution Jesus appointed to bring hope to the world."

That may have been the wrong thing to say to such a fiery young zealot, because I know a smile crept across my face as I issued my challenge, "Show me the church that wants to reach all people, and I'll show you the church where I'll invest my life."

To his credit, my pastor took my ideas to the board of elders and eventually offered me a full-time job aimed at broadening our church's relationship with its surrounding community. The new ministry venture that focused on our relationships beyond the four walls of the building was titled "Reach."

Looking back, I am confident Coach Gordon's advice was sound. I could not have achieved a position on the church staff without inviting the pastor into my process and securing his blessing. But looking back, if I had to do it again, I would take that advice one step further. I would seek the lead pastor's favor, and I'd sit down individually with each elder and staff person, as well as volunteer leaders in our community who I knew were influential.

I would try to invest the extra time in making sure all key leaders were repeatedly exposed to our vision for the community before the new efforts were announced to the congregation. By doing this, I'd be giving them the chance to ask questions and voice criticisms with me so that by the time the vision was being cast to attenders, the most influential leaders would be ready to take action and, I hoped, lead the way.

If you are not a pastor, an elder, or a staff person, though, be aware that as you seek to get buy-in from existing leaders, you may be walking on sensitive ground. Pastors, elders, or staff may sometimes feel threatened by the desire to take church beyond the four walls, as outreach could seem like an attempt to wrestle ministry away from their influence. But if it is fully understood, a *going* church does just the opposite. It invites church leaders to expand their influence, not diminish it. To lead a movement to take people beyond the building. To pastor not just the church but to extend their hearts and sense of mission toward the people surrounding it.

When pastors, staff, and elders own the idea of intentionally building relationships with all people in the community, it helps the goal of portable faith become less of a fringe idea championed by a small group of radicals, and it allows the act of going to become more mainstream—something that is part of our identity as a church.

Pastors, elders, and other church staff can support efforts to expand into the community by giving the vision a more widespread hearing. This may include announcing ministry opportunities from the pulpit, planning a sermon series around the value of going, adopting a statement of belief within the church's doctrine statements or core values, or tweaking the church's mission or vision to include emphasis on portable faith.

Support can also extend to a pastor's consciousness to preach with the lives of a diverse range of people in mind. For example, the pastor can subtly shift the way attenders perceive the church by beginning to use stories and examples that are not all about the majority ethnic or social group and that sometimes include people of different cultures or economic classes. (See exercise 7 about this exact art.)

On some days in my experience alignment with other leaders was almost seamless. One teaching pastor who eventually became my direct supervisor, for example, seemed to support my efforts early on. He even invited me to co-teach with him on this topic on a Sunday morning. This opportunity was not only validating to me as a staff person, that my work warranted sharing with the larger congregation, but it was the first time a woman had been given speaking time during the sermon slot in our church. The lead pastor also allowed me to lead a team of forty-five relief workers to Ground Zero immediately after the September 11 attacks. I have no doubt that had he not already bought into our larger vision to impact those outside our building, they would've never allowed me to do this, especially at twenty-three years of age.

There were also times when the goal of serving all people didn't seem to fully settle in with everyone who was teamed with me in ministry. At one point, we ordered customized leather journals to hold full-color notes that accompanied an upcoming sermon series. I was concerned, however, because the staff planned to sell the journals to attenders at a cost of thirty dollars each. And although most of our congregation could afford that price tag, a small number of attenders would have a hard time scraping up sixty dollars per couple.

Despite the concerns I raised, the price point wasn't taken into consideration when the journals were ordered. Or if it was considered, no plan was developed to offer alternatives. The beautiful leather journals, imprinted with our church's logo, arrived just a couple of days before the service during which the new sermon series would be launched.

As I imagined our attenders lining up to buy journals, all I could envision were the people who would stand off to the side, unable to participate: single mothers trying to work *and* find affordable day care, fathers who'd been laid off from work, college students burdened by rising tuition bills, and older people trying to make ends meet on a small pension.

Needless to say, I was frustrated. But mostly at myself. I knew that my other team members were good-hearted people trying to do something creative to engage our congregation in an upcoming sermon series. Clearly, they had no hidden agenda to purposefully leave out some attenders. But the fact that they didn't connect how the sale of an expensive journal could further marginalize people showed I had not communicated a community vision well enough to forge a truly united front. If I had tried to nurture more widespread buy-in,

I think more leaders would've discovered ways to own these values in the areas they oversaw. But since I didn't, I sometimes became frustrated or had to play catch-up in such situations.

Fortunately, every setback offered opportunity for growth. In the case of the journals, the oversight allowed some who served in our outreach ministries to show initiative to remedy the situation. At the last minute, they bought more affordable three-ring binders from a local office supply store and sold them as inexpensive alternatives to the more costly journals. The plain plastic version of the journal was nowhere near as nice, but it sold out. And not only was the less pricy version purchased by those who were strapped for cash, but many people who had gone through trainings in our ministry area also purchased the less costly version out of solidarity with others.

As you seek to influence the way your church perceives its mission, as you expand your church's reach into the surrounding community, it will be helpful to share your vision with and request support from as many leaders as possible. That would include all church elders, staff, administrators, secretaries, and receptionists, as well as volunteer leaders who oversee areas such as hospitality and ushering. You might also want to present your plans to those who run the social networks, websites, bulletins, or e-mail newsletters and those who facilitate trainings, orientations, or new member classes. The goal is to ask anyone who communicates about the church's identity to emphasize the church's desire to value the community, whether it be informing new members about volunteer opportunities, updating the church's Facebook friends about a graffiti cleanup, or prepping church greeters to intentionally welcome anyone and everyone, regardless of their appearance or background. The more leaders who understand and agree to support your cause in their area, the smoother the journey to go to your community will be.

Summary: If the leaders go to the community, the church will go to the community.

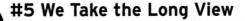

#5 We Take the Long View

In the beginning, we started programs and service projects—canned goods drives, Thanksgiving meal deliveries, and so forth—aimed at stirring good in our community and breathing fresh air into the dusty corners of our church. Although these efforts weren't yet attached to a year-round philosophy of ministry, they at least began physically shifting where our church logged its missional hours. And this was a start. After all, if you get your church attenders outside the building's four walls on a regular basis, you—by default—begin channeling some of your church's energy in an outward, *going* direction.

And so we went.

But even though the word *went* implies movement, we still weren't exactly going—present tense, continually, in the *-ing*, as-you-live sense. We were more or less just planning to be gone. Meaning we went and came back. Started and finished. Washed our hands. Packed up our gear. Reconvened for Sunday.

Outreach was packaged as a short-term project, and when it was completed, outreach was perceived as being done. Hence, our efforts often mobilized people to drop off faith the same way delivery persons might distribute pizzas before returning to the restaurant that dispensed them. Our attenders nurtured temporary good—deep cleaning the local homeless shelter or painting the low-income health clinic—that perhaps produced short-lived, pop-up, satellite expressions of church, but the efforts rarely seemed to nurture anything deeper or more lasting: inspired hearts or attentive consciences or lifestyles centered on going.

We ran a winter coat drive. After all the coats were collected, we distributed them. Then the coat drive was over. People felt good about being able to cross a task off their to-do list, and walked away feeling as though the Great Commission, or at least their part of it, was complete.

There was an implied but false finish line.

Although it felt good to help people and was satisfying to have a sense of completion when we took on short-term service projects, it also sometimes spurred a misguided belief that when a service project was done, the community's needs were met. The reality was that the children living in poverty in our community far outnumbered the quantity of coats we gathered. And there were kids going without coats on other Saturdays, not just the one closest to Thanksgiving, when we rallied to collect and distribute them. Not to mention, initiatives like coat drives treat only the symptoms of the issues that challenge our communities, without doing anything about the sources of the problem, such as unemployment, lack of affordable housing, addiction, or the breakdown of family.

The best church efforts, to the contrary, require more than just an hour or a day or a week of our time. Rather than plug people into times and places where they will do one service project, churches can better carry out the Great Commission by investing that same energy in teaching about Jesus' heart for all people, encouraging the expression of compassion, and raising awareness about unreached people groups and need in their communities.

The best church efforts don't do outreach; they encourage their attenders to live their faith in their communities every week of every year.

To help move our churches in this direction, we would be wise to stop providing a start and stop button that suggests that a lifestyle of care for the community can be turned on and off. Perhaps the best thing we can do to advance the church's growth along these lines, then, is to remove the illusion of the finish line.

Summary: The need to build relationships with the community is not over when your project ends.

#6 We Build Lasting Relationships

The people in our church were brilliant. They were leaders in the community: doctors, lawyers, CEOs, business owners, incredible parents, and so on. They knew how to nurture friendship. In fact, many of them had been maintaining relationships with one another for more than fifteen years. Some even shared history that stretched all the way back to their elementary school days.

But when the church provided opportunities for these same highly relational, socially savvy attenders to serve those outside the church, our efforts often failed to forge ongoing relationships with community members.

Attenders tended to feel detached from those in need, like helicoptered military personnel dropping emergency rations to people in a flood zone. *The help-in-a-bag lands, and then the helicopter flies away.*

We didn't hold to our usual standards for interaction, really trying to get to know community members, because often we didn't genuinely believe we'd see these people again. *We gave you a coat, a Christmas present, a Thanksgiving basket. But the reality is, you don't live in our neighborhood; you're not employed at our workplaces; our children aren't friends. Although we're not going to purposefully avoid you, this is probably, very literally, the only time in our lives we'll ever see you.*

I noticed the ineffectiveness with awe. It was like we had misplaced our usual friendship rhythm as soon as we stepped off the dance floor where we'd been performing all those years.

And yet we were applauded.

By some mix of grace and irony, most people—including my supervisors—were pleased enough with our efforts. There was a clear perception the church was doing more—*more* being an adjective that can far too easily masquerade as *good* or *right* in our culture.

43

But followers of the real, human, public-sphere-loving Jesus can't settle for just creating more for our churches to do. The point is not to be busy in Jesus' name. The point is to engage in things that help us and others become more like Jesus, to practice our faith in a way that opens our lives and others' lives to more of the fullness he came to bring.

Still, starting points are important. And getting into the community more regularly—even if at first it was via short-term projects that didn't forge lasting relationships—seemed to gradually propel our faith in a more going direction.

Faith slowly became a more portable concept. Yes, maybe we still treated belief as something of an object to some extent—an object intended to be passed across the counters on Sunday mornings or acquired by repeating a salvation prayer. Only now, after our first few steps into the community, we recognized our treasured object could also occasionally be slipped into someone's hand or maybe into coffee during a Thursday night service project or Saturday morning neighborhood cleanup.

It was a start.

Eventually, we found ways to organize our efforts to give us the best possible chance of building long-term relationships with the same families. When we collected school supplies, Thanksgiving meals, or coats, we intentionally circled back to the same families—thus expanding our interactions with them from one to half a dozen or so encounters per year.

But it was not just about year-round charity. It was about ongoing welcome and inclusion. As community members grew more comfortable with us, we invited them to join our small groups and our ministry teams and to serve alongside us via vacation Bible schools, classic car shows, and so on. And if the people we went to never felt comfortable enough with us or our church to attend weekend services, become members, or line up for baptisms, we tried to nurture friendship that carried faith to them, whether pulpits or altars were ever involved or not.

Although still immersed in tradition and although still connected to networks of other congregations, church became less about what earned religious applause or proved the congregation's growth and more about what carried Jesus to our community. There was something genuine and freeing in this, in learning to live and be church in a way that was not confined to a building or measured by the data a denomination or other body used to define growth.

Programmatically, we also began purposefully brainstorming ways to move beyond occasional encounters with community members to long-term relationships. This required us to step away from setting up short-term service projects and move toward recognizing and responding to opportunities for long-term relationship.

One way to foster this intentionality, I learned, is to pause and reflect every time someone brainstorms a way to serve the community. Before anyone moves to execute the idea, stop and ask yourselves a few questions so that you can refine the idea and present it in the strongest way possible:

- How many times will this ministry effort put you in contact with the same community members? Is it a one-time experience, or does it pave the way to interacting with people again and again over time?

- Does the ministry effort provide opportunity for church attenders to spend time talking and hanging out with community members, or will attenders spend the entire time serving and traveling and dropping things off?

- Will the location where the ministry effort takes place be a mutually comfortable meeting ground that encourages repeated interactions? Or will church attenders feel as though they're unnaturally forcing themselves into a community where they don't belong? And will those being ministered to regard church members as intrusive? What public meeting spaces are available that transcend social class, race, and background, such as community libraries, schools, and parks?

- Is there a natural way to invite the people we meet into long-term relationships with our community? Is there a church-affiliated play group or women's Bible study where single mothers could deepen their friendship with church attenders? Is there a church-affiliated softball league, a running group, or a men's lunch group that would provide natural relationships for the men the church meets? What long-term opportunities might be available to children?

One example of a long-term ministry opportunity that naturally arose in our context occurred during a conversation with a single mom who had been attending our church for a short time. Because her ex-husband lived out of state, she lamented that her son had very little exposure to positive male role models.

After thinking about the mom's words, I went to visit a pastor who had started a mentoring program between new believers and veterans of the faith. Although the program was never intended to match children with adults, the pastor was willing to adopt the model to invite a long-term attender to mentor the woman's son.

There were many ways we could've taken a stab at providing supportive role models to the woman's son, yet many of them would've been short-term. We could've purposefully introduced the little boy to an intentional children's ministry volunteer and asked the volunteer to keep a special eye out for the child. We could've invited the boy to some children's events, where he would've interacted with good role models as he played basketball or Frisbee with men from the church. But mentoring was something that lasted a minimum of one year and had the potential to stretch far beyond that.

Coach Wayne Gordon, the previously mentioned president of CCDA, suggested that mentoring was one of the most powerful and effective ways people of faith could invest in the well-being of their communities. Start with five-year-olds, Wayne always said, and mentor them every year. Support them, and provide encouragement, advice, and sometimes financial help through elementary school, middle school, and high school. And then, help them apply to and get through college. Don't just take the kids to Bible school or church; take them with you to run errands, to see how you deposit money into a bank account or how you budget for your shopping list at the grocery store. Live life alongside them. Take faith everywhere you go *and* let them go with you. They *go* as you *go*.

Geoffrey Canada, president and CEO of the Harlem Children's Zone in Harlem, New York, has figured out how to apply a similar principle to the field of education. The goal of his organization is to increase high school and college graduation rates among students in Harlem. To do this, he began tracking the educational progress of children who lived in one city block in the early 1990s, quickly expanding to serve and track the progress of children in a 24-block area by 1997. Their research showed them the importance of maintaining long-term relationships, so in 2000 they launched the Baby College, which started offering parenting classes to young mothers and fathers of newborns. In 2001, they launched an all-day preschool program called the Harlem Gems. They continued developing and improving programs for elementary, middle school, and high school students, even launching the College Success Office to offer extra support to students in college. They also have started health, financial, and community services aimed at whole neighborhoods, including adults and families.

Churches could take a lesson from the training and support his organization provides to parents and children—it commits to sticking with these families for life. Due to the success of the Harlem model, the area Geoffrey serves has already grown to ninety-seven blocks.

What would happen if churches adopted similar determination and perseverance? If they similarly embedded themselves in their immediate surroundings? If every church that currently invites its community to come, committed itself to supporting the children who lived in the blocks surrounding its building, and stuck with those children through adulthood, it would no doubt change the world in a way people like the woman mentioned in the first chapter of this book would be able to recognize.

Churches have a unique opportunity to put this principle into practice, which is perhaps why long-term church affiliation has been proved to offer greater benefits for health than many other interventions. Certainly, the truth and purpose found in Christ are responsible for people's transformation, but so is the way those truths are lived out in community. Counseling rarely lasts more than a couple of years. Support groups are often only a year long. But the local church, conceivably, will be there throughout residents' entire lives, providing not just one person to draw support from but an entire community that is invested in one another's well-being.

> *Summary: Always look for ways to turn a one-day interaction into a long-term relationship.*

#7 We Experience Meaningful Growth

Even though it became our goal to have long-term relationships with community members we served, to know them as friends and as potential contributors to our community, long-term relationships were not always possible. For example, one of the tasks I performed in my staff position was serving as a liaison between our attenders and the missionaries this church supported.

When a missionary couple was remodeling their field office in Brazil, we felt compelled to send a team of volunteers—and financial resources—to back their efforts. Although the couple had lived in our area twice, and some attenders knew them personally, many church attenders—including some who went on the trip—had no idea who they were or what they did.

Even though the group had a meaningful experience visiting and serving alongside the missionary couple and their community, a long-term in-person relationship was impractical. Most attenders who traveled to their home didn't have the financial resources to make return trips to Brazil throughout their lives.

In this case, a pastor who led the trip and I did two things:

First, we tried to prep team members to view the experience as one that was more concerned with their development than service to the Brazilian community. While the hope was to set aside our usual routines to help complete a project that would benefit the region, we tried to set our minds on how we could expand our understanding of the world and learn from people we were going to meet. We administered personality tests and encouraged participants to focus on what we could learn about operating as a team and engaging tough physical labor, long travel, and limited accommodations with people who had different gifts and temperaments. How could God use the experience to make everyone involved a more attentive, compassionate, and responsive human being?

The benefit of doing ministry in a brief period of time is that it sometimes creates an enhanced laboratory for personal learning. Our focus is strong because we've set aside all our typical life distractions. We often spend more time in prayer and spiritual practices. And our attentiveness is generally heightened because we are so fascinated by all the new things to which we are exposed. We can't help comparing and contrasting the part of the world we are visiting with the part of the world we live in. This sometimes prompts reflection on our values and priorities and stirs resolve to make lifestyle changes when we return home.

Of course, not everyone can go to Brazil to benefit from this growing experience. For this reason we began offering the exercises at the end of this book, which seek to expose attenders to those they may not know, to set new focus, and to raise awareness and help people respond within our community.

Second, in addition to seeing short-term ministry opportunities as developmental for all involved, we tried to maintain awareness of what these missionaries were doing in Brazil, even after the team returned home. I began including occasional updates in newsletters that went out to our church, added a website tab that featured them, asked one missionary to speak to some of our ministry volunteers on a conference call, and put inserts in our bulletin updating people on what they were up to now. In this way, we invited our people to continue to learn from and be influenced by both the missionaries and their community.

We invested our money and energy not in an attempt at heroics but from a desire to grow ourselves and our long-term relationships.

Summary: Even though our efforts may benefit others, focus participants' attention on growing themselves.

#8 We Value All People in the Community

The best relationships usually form naturally. After two parties are introduced, they often continue to cross paths until a connection gradually develops between them. Similarly, it makes sense for a church to adopt a normal, healthy pace when seeking to build relationships with its community. The church shouldn't expect relationships to develop overnight. Perhaps one or two exceptional cases will emerge where people or organizations become immediately smitten with your congregation. But in most cases, it will likely take months and years to develop trust between your church attenders and those outside your church, particularly people groups that may feel vulnerable because of previously wounding religious experience or their position on society's margins.

In a new friendship, a first encounter with an individual would likely be casual, perhaps involving a brief introduction or some light small talk. In view of this, we began looking for comfortable starting points for the church to build authentic, balanced relationships with the community.

One idea we tried at the church where I worked was creating coloring pages that captured ideas central to our beliefs, such as "All people matter to God" or "Relationships are vital for health." One, for example, displayed a collection of children who appeared to be from different cultures, with different levels of ability. Then we distributed stacks of these to area waiting rooms where children might be present.

Obviously, not every office will feel comfortable placing material in the lobby that could be viewed as religious, but many privately owned businesses—from pediatricians' private practices to oil change experts—welcomed them. We started by placing the papers in the waiting rooms of businesses owned or operated by people in our church or by friends of people in our church. But even many strangers were not opposed to letting us provide coloring sheets for their child clients or the children of their customers.

Each coloring sheet contained a note that said something like "We've provided this coloring sheet because we want our community to know we care," along with our church logo. The paper didn't include the church address or service times because the purpose was not to recruit members but to express caring. It did, however, include our website so they could get to know us more if they chose.

Another thing we did was to send welcome notes to babies born in our community. We weren't able to acquire the address of every baby born, but often the paper listed new parents whose addresses could be found in the phone book or other public records. On the front of the card, we drew a design with the words "It Takes a Village to Raise a Child." Then, on the inside, volunteers wrote a congratulatory note that said something like "We heard you have an addition to your family, and we wanted to take a minute to welcome your new little one to our community. If you would like a free children's Bible for your newborn, please stop by our church anytime during office hours."

Again, nothing was included that invited them to our church services or asked them to review Scripture verses. The fact that they would be welcome if they ever came was implied. The point was just to say, we the church and our God care about you.

Another idea that worked well was starting an exchange where we listed needs submitted to the church. For example, a teenage mother in her first apartment needed furniture. A family whose home burned down needed clothing of certain sizes. A pair of twins needed winter coats. A person with special needs was looking for a weekly ride to the grocery stores.

But thanks to the leadership of one motherly volunteer who initiated the exchange, it was not limited to people perceived as financially disadvantaged. A middle-class family of long-term attenders was looking for a nanny to watch their kids. An established retiree needed a house sitter while she was in Florida for the winter. Someone's dog had puppies that needed homes. At the time, we listed these needs on a monthly newsletter that we made available at the church information table, although now it might make more sense to place it online. In almost every case, people in the church came forward to help without the church needing to raise money to meet the listed needs. A simple sheet of paper that provided information to our community enabled Acts 2 exchanges without formal programming.

This exchange didn't change anyone's life, but it did make a small practice of saying that we care. We care even if you don't come to our church. And we're willing to take a few minutes to make your need known and to invite people to help.

> *Summary: Allow the church's relationship with the community to take a natural pace that shows you value the people in it.*

#9 We Value What the Community Values

Another way we showed the community we valued them was to attempt to purposefully value what residents valued. Although this philosophy of valuing what the community values was already in place at our church prior to my time there, the church had largely limited its community involvement to popular mainstream activities that tended to be predominantly attended by the white middle class.

In our city, for example, there was a strong tradition of patriotism. At a yearly event called the Civil War Muster, thousands of residents turned out to reenact the Civil War or watch the production. In thinking about this one year, a small team decided to make a gesture of value by giving away handheld American flags to participants. On another occasion, our church entered a hot-air balloon and offered activities for children during a well-known regional event called the Hot Air Jubilee.

Our new emphasis on building relationships outside our four walls allowed us to expand on this practice by seeking ways to value every people group known to be living in our city rather than being present only at events serving the ethnic, economic, and social groups represented by the majority of our attenders.

For example, our manufacturing city had largely supported Detroit's auto industry, and another long-standing interest revolved around cars. Our church had a legacy of expressing solidarity with car-loving residents before my staff position was established. This legacy inspired us to host a classic car show and also to participate in a racing event called Mini Indy. In addition to these popularly attended events, a couple who served as small-group leaders eventually developed a vision to reach out to NASCAR fans in our community, which was only a half hour or so from the Michigan International Speedway.

The couple was able to create an event for race fans who couldn't afford tickets or who weren't otherwise able to watch the race in person. They arranged with the church's technology team to broadcast the race on the big screen in our auditorium and provided free refreshments, as well as generous door prizes donated by area businesses, to those in attendance.

Doing this type of relationship-building was so enjoyable that at one point, we maintained a small team of volunteers whose sole goal was to create a positive presence at as many community events as they could. You should've heard the ideas we came up with: giving away pencils during back-to-school shopping days, providing free gift wrapping on the last day before Christmas (no donations accepted!), making Polaroid souvenirs at Daddy-Daughter dances, giving away water at a street fair, or doing face painting at a rec center's carnival.

Our presence at these events occasionally resulted in people visiting our church, but that was not the intention. The intention was to shake people's hands on behalf of our church and our God. To help them know our names and to communicate in a brief interaction that we cared. To live and be church in a way that valued each group within our community.

> *Summary: Spend time with the community by intentionally doing what the community does and valuing what the community values.*

#10 We Value Who the Community Values

Along with valuing what the community values, there is wisdom in trying to express value for the people in your community.

Ideas for doing this could include:

- hosting a thank-you dinner for your community's firefighters, police, or EMT workers.
- giving a small token of thanks to teachers, either at the beginning or the end of the school year.
- placing flags on the graves of your community's veterans.

- handing out flowers to women who are lunching downtown on Mother's Day.

- taking brownies or cupcakes to the city staff.

- handing out lemonade to road construction workers.

- taking hot chocolate to parking attendants, bell ringers, or others who do their jobs outside in cool weather.

- Setting up days devoted to specific random acts of kindness, such as Take a Cup of Starbucks to Your Barber Day.

- Encouraging your children's ministry to make cards for a group of people in your community—librarians or crossing guards, for example.

Again, the idea is not to hold some type of religious ceremony, to deliver evangelical literature, or even to recruit new members. The point is to offer sincere thanks and appreciation to the people who serve your community as an act of love.

Oddly enough, though, our goodwill gestures were often well received and pleasantly surprising. These acts often generated good word of mouth, identifying us as a "church who cares" in the community. And on some occasions, these acts even drew new visitors to church services.

Summary: Show how much you care about the community by loving those who care for it.

#11 We Prepare Carefully and Thoughtfully

Along with intentionally trying to be a positive presence in the community, we can use wisdom to try to avoid a bad first impression.

When my husband and I lived in a busier, urban neighborhood, I still remember the day a prominent church in town came to our block to do a service project. What tipped us off was the influx of white people, because on most days we were among just a few Caucasians in the area. But this day, there was a large group of mostly middle-aged white people walking through the neighborhood, each with a trash bag in his or her hand.

The city block had never seen so many polo shirts in all its years combined!

As we watched these well-dressed residents pick up litter around our neighborhood, a task that inarguably needed to be done, my husband and I noted their polite demeanor and friendly waves as they worked. And when they left, we celebrated that the neighborhood had had a nice face-lift!

But we quickly learned not everyone on the block viewed the church's stop as a positive one.

Many of our African American neighbors had a different impression. And it went something like this: "Who do these rich white people think they are, driving in from their suburban neighborhoods to tell us how to clean our neighborhood?"

In hearing their response, church members might have responded defensively, "Well, they're responsible for how they respond. We did it with good hearts, and if they don't have the ability to be grateful for our investment, that's their problem."

There's probably truth in both parties' impressions. But if the point of our work is to show our surrounding communities that our church cares, and instead we accidentally make them feel judged, we haven't accomplished the purpose.

Love that makes people feel harmed rather than legitimized or cared for isn't loving, just as help is not sincerely help unless it can be received as such.

As a staff person responsible for building relationships with our community, I committed to attenders that our church would try to support all their corporate outreach ideas, but I asked them to share ideas before acting on them so we could work together on how to do the most amount of good while incurring the least amount of damage. Because of this safeguard, we would have the chance to fine-tune plans for a neighborhood cleanup or similar project before we engaged it as a congregation. Not only did this open up the leadership and planning process to diverse groups within the church, but having different perspectives at the idea table helped us come up with more rounded and sensitive ideas.

For example, for a neighborhood cleanup like the one the well-to-do church sent to our urban community, someone in the planning group might suggest choosing a shared cleanup site such as a community playground, so our people were never picking up trash out of residents' yards uninvited. And then maybe before we went out, the planning team would make flyers that invited the community to join us in cleaning up the playground. Maybe we'd send a couple of people to area businesses or even door-to-door to post the flyers and invite community members to come to the park to help out.

Another suggestion that might arise would be to ask another church, one that is geographically closer to the park or one attended by the same social and cultural groups who most use the park, to cosponsor the playground cleanup. A suburban church like ours could invite an urban church or neighborhood to help clean up a more suburban park on a different day. This approach reduces the chance of appearing to be followers of Christ who have a superiority complex, invites us to get to know our fellow residents as equals, and brings groups of diverse people together for the common good.

Summary: Before choosing to act, spend time reflecting on how to love the community in a way that can be received as love.

#12 We Are Persistent and Patient in Encouraging Change

I've read that you can tell a lot about what a person values by looking at what he or she spends time and money on. I think we could use these same indicators to learn a lot about a church as well.

Imagine archaeologists digging through the rubble of your current church building one thousand years from now, and they stumble onto a log of how your staff or attenders spent their time. Every service, every potluck, every small group, every Bible study, every hour the cleaning team or the hospitality team or the greeter team got together to meet. And then imagine the researchers compare the total of those hours invested in building or maintaining in-house ministries to the total number of hours the church spent outside the building. By studying how your church used its time, what would the archaeologists determine about your church's identity? Based on the data, would they likely conclude you valued going to the world?

What if, along the way, they found your church's detailed accounting records? If they studied the money spent on mortgage payments, electricity, sound equipment, music, props, books, snacks, and everything else that must be purchased to conduct ministry to weekend and midweek attenders? And what if they then compared that total to the amount of money that went to developing ministries or purchasing items that benefited residents beyond the four walls of your church building? Based on the data, would they likely conclude you valued going to the world?

I'm not suggesting that a certain percentage of time or money must be set aside for programs outside your doors. But I do remember as a child thinking it seemed a little bit odd when church leaders proudly announced that they gave 7 percent to foreign missions or 4 percent to local missions (or some other similar number). My little brain always quickly calculated that meant 11 percent was going to the community or "world," while 89 percent went to run the church. When I got older and began to say this aloud, I quickly learned it was an unpopular thing to say.

But it still strikes me as very opposite, although difficult to reverse, of what Jesus intended. If the main idea was to go to the world, how did we end up designating only a small amount of money to expanding that purpose?

Some churches have taken measures to keep their overhead low by renting space rather than buying, sharing the same building among several congregations, or employing bivocational pastors. However, most churches won't be able to responsibly reverse the way they allocate 100 percent of their time and money overnight.

Even so, churches can do some things to gradually shift their focus to include a stronger emphasis on going:

- Add ideas about faith's portable nature, about going, into core values, websites, membership manuals, and informational brochures.

- Encourage and recognize the service of people who serve in the community as much as you publicly applaud those who serve the church. Perhaps hold a ceremony to acknowledge the woman who selflessly gave ten years to the church nursery. Take the time that same night to recognize the guy who coached kids' soccer for ten years at the community rec center.

- Hold small-group leader trainings that prepare people to lead groups that serve your attenders, and invest in trainings that help people nurture community outside your church's four walls via office book clubs, play groups, Super Bowl parties, neighborhood barbecues, and so forth. You'd be surprised how many people would enjoy learning about how to be a better friend and neighbor.

- Try to make sure the building is used as much as possible if you're going to devote the money to paying a mortgage on a building. Do you have a gym? Open it to a local middle school that doesn't have enough room for all its teams to practice. Are there substance abuse or support groups that could offer their services in one of your classrooms? Could you open the sanctuary during limited hours for people who need a quiet place to pray? Aim to be a seven-day-a-week church.

- Determine to allocate a larger percentage of time and money this year than you designated last year for ministries that happen outside your building. If you were at 7 percent, go to 8, 10, or 15 percent.

- Set a goal to start a certain number of ministries that will serve people who do not attend weekend services.

- Reserve a certain number of weekend services, classes, and small groups per year to encourage and prepare people to carry faith to the community.

- Determine to create space in services to share what the church is doing outside its building. Let those who participate in service projects, mission trips, or ministry efforts to the community talk about what they learned. Interview community members on stage or via video, and ask them to share how they joined with or interacted with church attenders during an outreach experience.

- Offer orientation to serving your surrounding community, and encourage as many congregation members as possible to attend. Most important, provide training and teaching for church leaders as they influence the larger body of attenders and often shape initiatives that represent your church to those who are not members. (Exercises that could be used for orientations and trainings are provided at the end of this book.)

- Recruit volunteer leaders, or if you have the funds, hire a staff person who has the heart and ability to champion community relationships for your church.

One additional word of wisdom: whether or not you can allocate more money to serve the community, always keep in perspective that money and tangible resources aren't the most important things you have to offer. Hope, peace, and purpose found in God are worth far more than any amount of money you could offer. And even if you don't have the financial resources to help someone in need, it can be helpful sometimes to just offer to listen or to have a cup of coffee together in an act of friendship.

To hold the value of money and community in balance, when people came to request financial help from our church, we asked them to fill out a short application that included information on service times as well as other opportunities to become more involved with our church community if they so desired. This included boxes for them to check to indicate whether they wanted us to match them with someone to provide financial or job coaching or professional counseling and whether they would like more information on available classes, small groups, and ministry areas in which they could participate free of charge.

> **Summary: Churches rarely reinvent themselves overnight, so look for ways to shift energy and resources gradually toward the community.**

#13 We Give and Receive

Sometimes, we reach out to others out of duty, out of allegiance to a higher power, or out of a strong sense of discipline. This is not necessarily bad. The concept of sacrificing our personal preferences for the sake of others often gets lost in our rights-happy culture, but deferring our desires for the good of the whole can be a genuinely noble act.

However, it's wise for anyone involved in ministry to at least occasionally admit the following: sometimes I do things that appear to be for other people, but they are actually for myself.

Sometimes this self-interest is healthy. Part of the reason we serve or reach out is because, as we discussed earlier, it can be spiritually developmental. When we practice being generous, the act of giving of ourselves grows new habits inside us. We become what we're doing: compassion, generosity, grace.

But sometimes, if church leaders and attenders are honest, we engage others because we need to be needed. Most of us probably don't mind playing the hero part sometimes. And even this is not all bad because it's natural and even right to feel good about contributing to the community in which we live. These good feelings show that we are aware of our connectedness to those around us and that we understand how our actions can affect others for good or bad.

The tricky part, though, is keeping in the forefront of the mind that serving the community is not a one-way exchange. *We* are not the sole givers, and *they* are not the sole receivers. Our interaction stirs good for all of us.

It's so important to be aware of the hero complex that lies in each of us because the shadow side of a hero complex is a martyr complex. Anyone who ignores inner struggles while striving to matter and to be applauded risks becoming *that* person—that person who is constantly telling everyone else how much he or she did for the whole. The person whose fingers are always cramped because she just spent hours knitting a blanket for a newborn. The person who is always exhausted from staying up until 2:00 a.m. putting decorations together for an event his church is hosting.

It's wise, then, for churches to occasionally do heart checks, to use meeting times to remind our volunteers and ourselves that stories are best told to transmit meaning, to share our source of good—what God is doing in our lives. It's helpful to resolve together to consciously pause whenever we're telling a story about some act of service we've just completed and to ask ourselves why we are talking about it. Are we telling a story to capture meaning or learning? Or are we sharing it to impress others, search out affirmation, or improve our religious status?

When we maintain awareness that we are not the only ones—or the *main* ones or the *indispensable* ones—contributing to the church or to the community, when we remember every person both gives and receives, we protect not only those we serve but also the condition of our hearts. It frees us. It frees us from the illusion of superiority, from being workaholics who never take a break or never accept help from others, and it frees us from arrogance that can destroy our personalities and diminish others.

By taking this posture of humility and seeking to recognize the contributions of others, we may even be surprised by how much is invested by some people we didn't previously believe contributed.

Maybe we'll discover that the things we thought were so good, the things we thought we were going to bring to the rest of the world, weren't even that good.

Maybe we're the rich, unhappy guys checking in before 9:00 a.m. and staying two or four or six hours later than 5:00 p.m. clock-out time. Maybe we're spending all day faxing things, returning billions of e-mails, sitting through meetings bored out of our minds.

Maybe we're going home to fertilize and mow and weed-whack our lawns because we feel pressure to keep up with the magazine-cover-worthy yard of our neighbors and to paint the trim on our houses because we don't want it to depreciate in value since the mortgage payment seems to be a huge anchor around our necks.

Maybe we're spending our entire day running our kids around to their eleven elective appointments—to soccer and violin, even though they hate soccer and violin.

Or maybe we're sinking huge chunks of life into cleaning all the clothes we have, ironing them, dry-cleaning them, hanging them on hangers. Dusting and mopping and vacuuming that extra five hundred square feet. Or weeding gardens until our hands bleed, trying to keep up with a home improvement show we watch.

When we take a step back, maybe helping some "poor" person who has none of these privileged possessions become more like us and our friends isn't as genius as it seems. Maybe we were actually just getting ready to snap the handcuffs over their wrists, to attach a fifty-pound weight to their ankles.

I have often wondered if I had the choice between the condition of heart of a child dying of AIDS in Africa and that of a CEO earning millions, which would I want? Whose emotions? Whose innocence? Whose peace? Whose vitality?

Who would I want to be inside and out?

I am not suggesting I would dismiss having the health of the CEO, or that starvation, poor health care, or disease should be dismissed. They shouldn't be. By God, they shouldn't be.

I'm just suggesting that maybe those who struggle, those who are deemed have-nots by our culture, aren't the *before* and we aren't the *after*.

We know that, though, right?

We've picked up that everyone in Hollywood isn't happy. We've ascertained that money and status just as often lure people into addiction to more money, drugs, public approval, depression, and starving themselves to obtain a certain body image.

But are our own values necessarily superior to the values of those we serve?

Maybe we're sitting in our living rooms thinking we must have the newest glossy hair product so people will fawn over us just like the person in the commercial who is sitting in an open convertible, surrounded by friends at the beach who are laughing uproariously. Maybe this commercialization has influenced us to stockpile hundreds of half-used beauty products in our cabinets and closets, none of which ever deliver the feeling we seek.

If so, who is better off? The people who buy the products, or those who can't? Who is brainwashed, and who needs to be freed?

There's a funny reality when it comes to money. Sometimes people don't need to break into your house to take your possessions. Sometimes, when you keep those possessions, you rob yourself of just as much, especially when you may be keeping them at the expense of your sanity, your freedom, or your ability to rest and enjoy life. Sometimes even when you're feasting during a famine, the real person who is starving is you.

People with wealth often work long hours to be able to maintain their possessions and protect and insure what they have. They buy security systems, electronic gates, fire and flood insurance, guns. On their worst nights, after watching too much *CSI* or *Law and Order*, they feel at risk in their own homes, knowing that their wealth would make them the target of any would-be thieves in the area. Maybe that was why Jesus said to sell your possessions—because, when you do that, the prisoner you're freeing is you.

Maybe people who have less are sometimes freer than those who have more. Maybe people with less formal education sometimes have just as much or more to teach. Maybe someone who works in a blue-collar job sometimes does more good for the human race than someone with a white-collar job.

Maybe the world would be a better place if people fancied themselves as learners as often as they fancied themselves teachers.

*Summary: **Fight signs of accidental heroism that suggest you are always the giver, and they are always the receivers.***

 **#14 We Obey Christ's Commandment**

When I first started to encourage churches to develop relationships with diverse people in their communities, I sometimes encountered resistance to the idea.

One protest I often heard was, "People like to associate with their own kind. No matter what we do, other people groups aren't going to attend our church. Other races and cultures are attracted to worship with their own kind, in their own style."

And there's some truth in this analysis. People *are* drawn to familiarity. And it does make sense, that—whether grouped by social or economic class or by any other feature—people might be drawn to churches where they feel best understood.

But the problem is these longed-for "understanding" or "comfortable congregations" don't always exist. In fact, if we allow an individual's or group's level of comfort to dissuade us from pursuing relationship with them, there are some who will never have Christ extended to them. Whether a person's identity is shaped by the color of their skin, their cultural traditions, their lifestyle, their sexuality, their eating habits, their education, their family makeup, their criminal record, or any other determiner, some people groups in some communities won't find a church that is customized to their background or identity or comfort. And as a result, there are groups who will feel marginalized and excluded from *all* churches. When this is the case, the only way certain groups will find a faith community is if a church of apparently unlike people extends a welcome.

And there is hope even in this scenario. After all, if you follow the Bible or even history, God has proven he has quite a bit of reach outside of people's comfort zones. In fact, you might say his M.O. usually leads through decidedly uncomfortable territory.

Noah endured a worldwide flood, Moses survived a scorching desert, David withstood a threatening giant, Daniel faced the claws and teeth of lions, and Esther challenged a madman who plotted to extinguish her people. And that's only to scratch the surface of Old Testament discomfort, which in itself only leads to a New Testament full of similarly stretching stories. The rich man was told to sell his possessions, the woman at the well was called beyond her history of unfaithfulness, Paul was challenged to leave his violent tradition of religious extremism, and Peter was instructed to go to the Gentiles.

Christianity's history is in fact far better described as uncomfortable than comfortable. And historically, followers of God are much better described as a mismatched collection of *unlike* people than a group of similar people who flocked to one another out of comfort.

Fortunately, discomfort can be transcended in modern times as well.

A truly useful and inviting faith community can still attract people from across the racial, economic, and social spectrums. This is certainly proven by the small number of exceptional churches whose diverse demographics transcend cultural norms. But it's also evidenced by simple faith and logic.

As I point out in the diversity chapter of my first book, *Dear Church*, even though people typically gravitate toward those like themselves (and even that is perhaps arguable generationally), there are plenty of exceptions to that rule even in nonreligious contexts. When people deem a place or gathering valuable to them, whether it be for entertainment benefit or for general usefulness, normal barriers seem to come down. Walmart or major league baseball or certain concerts, for example, draw people from all over the social, racial, and economic spectrums. A person of faith would certainly have to conclude, then, that big box stores, athletic stadiums, and the music labels are not accomplishing something that God himself cannot do, right?

But beyond the practical argument, I think a "people want to worship with their own kind" resistance reflects a lack of thoughtfulness about the Great Commission. It may sometimes even reflect a dismissive attitude toward *going*.

After all, Jesus never said the act of going into all the world was a practical or easily executed one. And he certainly never suggested the whole world would respond favorably to our efforts. In both cases, in fact, he stated exactly the opposite. "In this world you will have trouble. But take heart! I have overcome the world" (John 16:33). Whether or not people feel naturally drawn to us, then, seems to have little bearing on Jesus' instruction.

We go not based on the degree to which we think faith should be carried to the world, but on what Jesus told us to do. We go because we've realized a bedrock truth: that it is impossible to reach the whole world if we refuse to go to people unlike ourselves. And we go because we have faith that the outcome of following God's divine, supernatural intentions is better than the outcome of what we believe to be possible or comfortable.

Not to mention that the worst-case scenario, in which diverse people don't choose to come to our local church as a result of our efforts, seems to have little relevance to Jesus' end goal. His aim was not to get people to come to weekend services, it was not to grow one specific congregation into a super church or to convert community members to one culture's worship style. He wanted us to go so all

67

people could be exposed to his teachings and invited to experience the life God intended for us. We were never mandated to drag the world to church buildings. We were only urged to disciple them and then to gather with them in fellowship.

When modern-day, Western churches embrace going to the world, even if some of the world never chooses to sit in a brick box marked by pews and a steeple, the walls of church buildings will become irrelevant, the lines between the denominations will become less prominent, and followers of Jesus will present a more united front capable of carrying faith to an entire planet.

As churches begin to embrace this ideal, it is of course realistic to expect to encounter obstacles.

When people resist the idea that churches should intentionally build relationships with diverse people, sensitivity is required. Beyond just discomfort, mingling amongst unknown people like Jesus did can be scary and unpredictable. As a result, church leaders and attenders challenged to reach diverse groups may fear their previous work, which focused on their own race or economic class, is being diminished or judged. They may worry that carrying faith beyond their existing group will require too much of them. They may be concerned that diverse people will bring change to their preferred way of doing church, that they may lose or have to share influence with others, or that people unlike themselves will bring tension, controversy, and even danger.

However, if we truly believe what we say we do, then the discomfort, the difficulty, the tension, and the fear must take a backseat to faith and possibility.

Certainly we could make pros-and-cons lists, look at crime statistics, and conduct a cost-benefit analysis to make self-preserving decisions, but in the end, we would not be able to guarantee our own safety no matter whom our church serves. Nor would we be able to guarantee that if we resist change, if we hunker down in worship with the same hundred people with whom we've been worshipping for twenty years, that our own way of church will survive. The evolutions of church history, in fact, suggest otherwise.

If it's true, then, that any mix of things can create dangers or difficulties that we ourselves cannot even anticipate, and if all options include unavoidable risk, then doesn't it make sense to choose the risk associated with serving at the pleasure of the Creator?

Unfortunately, much of where we allow our churches to go—how we approve new initiatives, appoint leadership, allocate budgets, or design services—is based on our definition of success and what we've allowed to creep into the fine print of that definition.

Jesus told his followers to get the good news to every creature; to disciple, to baptize, and to teach the world to align themselves with his teachings.

What if we used these parting instructions to his disciples as a filter for our churches?

What if when someone proposed a new idea for our church, we immediately forced it through these filters—Does it go to the world? Does it disciple? Does it baptize? Does it teach obedience to Jesus' teachings?

What if we committed to stop making decisions about our churches based on any criteria other than these?

Too often we take on additional pressures.

We envision success as maintaining our programs. As making sure we have enough musicians and worship team members scheduled to cover the next six months of services. As having a higher attendance this week than last week or last month or last year. As having the money to expand our buildings. As having gigantic offerings and record-setting fundraising drives. As staying up-to-date technologically. As being well-branded. As making sure we—and anyone we let onstage—present ourselves in a culturally admirable way. The list goes on and on.

Sometimes we allow these secondary criteria to creep into the fine print of our definition of success. We begin to judge ourselves by them. Suddenly, we are drowning in excess work! We have to keep the music team scheduled, we have to court wealthy donors, we have to advertise so we can set an Easter attendance record, we have to keep all these programs spinning!

And worse yet, with all these secondary criteria looming over us, we begin feeling bad about our inability to perform.

But if Jesus walked into your building and wandered around observing all the activities going on in your children's ministries, all the events put on for your youth, all the creative hoopla that happens on your church stage—you know what he would be looking for?

Going.

Discipling.

Baptizing.

And teaching people to align themselves with what he taught.

For too long, success in the church world has been confused with earning the approval of a board of elders, a lead pastor, a denomination, or a group of funders. But once we realize that the fine print below our definition of success is bloated and impairing our movement, we can cut it loose. Then what can badger us? What can hold us prisoner? What can heap accusations of failure on our efforts?

Typos on the screen? Feedback in the mic? A summer attendance drop?

No.

Next to going, discipling, baptizing, and teaching what Jesus taught, all of this loses its power.

And my guess is if churches made their center point going, discipling, teaching, and baptizing, they would no longer feel dominated by the workload that comes with sustaining all those programs. It would create space and energy to approach the uncomfortable, difficult, and rewarding adventure of going.

Summary: We go not because we know people will always respond. We go because we are told to go.

Chapter Four

How to Train the Portable Church

Encouraging Reflection vs. Training to Task

Many churches begin from the same point we did.

They start by identifying the most pressing needs in their community—homelessness, juvenile delinquency, teenage pregnancy, often whatever social problems have most dominated recent local headlines. And then, using conventional common sense, they begin recruiting church attenders to serve in a list of new programs that address those needs. They launch after-school tutoring programs, take dinners to the homeless shelter, and collect diapers for the local women's health center.

It's good, and fairly simple, to match people to specific programs—to serve in a local shelter, your food pantry, or your clothes closet. After a brief orientation meeting and a little on-the-job training, they'll quickly pick up the necessary skills to advance the goals of the program. In a clothes closet, for instance, they'll learn how to sift donations, what to do with sub-par items that can't be distributed, and how to organize pick-up or deliveries most efficiently. And, of course, results seem immediate. Church attenders will master their particular roles. And the addition of each newly trained person will help fill the clothing closet schedule and ensure the program can be sustained over time.

71

But despite how intuitive it seems, in trying this approach, we quickly found short-term good can become the enemy of the long-term best.

Training to a specific program, in our case, often produced only temporary benefits. Trainees brought about noticeable, tangible positives, such as raking an older adult's yard or helping a person who never completed high school earn a GED. But in the genuine good accomplished, the programs almost always failed to invite the people we served into any kind of sustainable relationship.

We also observed that when we only trained volunteers to staff a single program, we sometimes accidentally created single-minded attenders who poured their time and energy into just one pet cause. This sometimes seemed to transform them into activists for a particular social issue rather than people concerned with being like Jesus or going as Jesus went.

We came to believe that while training toward a specific program or ministry had positive impact, and was sometimes necessary, there were more transformative and balanced ways of helping people prepare to live their faith in the community.

We found there was value, for example, in having attenders go through a more open-ended and reflective orientation to the community before they joined a specific program and trained to do a particular task. This initial orientation was devoted to getting to know our community and sharing in experiences that raised awareness or empathy toward needs or people groups in our area. It also included guided reflection about how God might want each of us, as individuals and as a congregation, to build relationships and respond to need.

Starting with a broader, more open-ended orientation added another step to our processes and thus took longer and required more energy of us. However, the awareness and sensitivity that it nurtured served both the attenders and the church far more deeply and broadly than our program-specific training.

The additional value was almost immediately obvious. What if an attender who goes through this reflection process never signs up for any of the ministries that fall under the "outreach" area, for instance? What if they never go on a relief trip or sign up to mentor teenagers who need a positive role model?

It doesn't matter.

If they serve in another area of the church—sound team or hospitality, for instance—they will carry with them a heightened attentiveness and sensitivity to the community that will likely impact their perspective and actions as they serve. Maybe, for example, they will be particularly supportive of the single mom who volunteers on their team or perhaps they will go out of their way to be especially welcoming to a visitor from a different race or economic group.

If orientation graduates take what they have learned to other departments within the church, they don't subtract from an outreach department, they actually help strengthen how outreach happens by spreading the emphasis throughout the congregation. In this way, portable faith doesn't become the mantra of just a handful of volunteers in one ministry area, it can become a value that beats from the hearts of those stationed across the entire church.

Additionally, because the guided reflection is geared more toward the attender's development rather than meeting a specific need or staffing a particular program, the insights are applicable to the attender's entire life. Even if they choose not to serve in any ministry in the church, even if they move out of state and begin attending a different church, even if they stop going to church altogether, the principles they pick up from this training can impact the way they perceive the gospel, how seriously they regard the Great Commission, and how they express their faith in their communities for years to come. This orientation is not just geared toward teaching people a skill, such as how to write receipts for those who donate clothes, it aims at increased awareness: seeing opportunity for relationship and responding to need in ordinary life.

It's tempting to train to a short-term good, such as filling open spots in the soup kitchen. But it serves the global church well when we try to nurture habits and practices that prepare people for a lifetime of going to the world, wherever in the world they may be.

Summary: Rather than training to a specific task that prepares people to serve in one kind of ministry, help raise their awareness of the opportunity to build relationships in their community throughout their lives.

Let Passion Lead You

Here's how many churches, including ours, staffed ministries that might qualify as outreach: the church would make a list of empty posts in existing programs and then recruit volunteers to fill these spots. Logical enough, right? However, after observing how attenders participated and grew within our ministry, we decided to depart from the standard way of recruiting to need. And we tried a new approach that could've tanked our ministry area's volunteer base if it failed.

After providing information about our community, creating opportunities to get out in the public sphere, and encouraging our volunteers to reflect on these experiences, we decided to stop trying to just plug people into programs based on our own desperation. Instead, we invited our people to take ownership alongside us in dreaming about how ministry would unfold outside our church.

Here's how this worked:

When people completed our initial orientation, which was made up of a combination of the exercises at the end of this book, we asked attenders to try to identify the people groups, needs, or causes they were most passionate about. What ministry ideas or opportunities for relationship were stirring inside them that they felt needed to be brought to expression? If attenders couldn't easily pinpoint a type of ministry that drew them in, or was at least a natural fit, we asked them to take a few weeks to see if any specific vision attached itself to their spirits. Then we followed up with them a few weeks later and asked.

While some people weren't moved by a particular vision and were willing to serve in any ministry that served the community, there were always a handful of attenders who could not get a specific ministry idea out of their heads. No matter where they went, a particular group or objective—single moms or homelessness, high school dropouts or clean water—seemed to keep surfacing. And no matter how much time passed, the same idea kept returning to them.

When these passions surfaced for attenders, it was the church staff's pleasure, at that point, to step back as the inventing or controlling entity and to empower attenders to bring what God was doing in them to expression.

Yes, this kind of open-handed training sometimes resulted in the formation of programs, but the programs ebbed and flowed with how God's spirit moved ideas in our community. The resulting ministries represented causes that were selected based on the burdens God placed on the hearts of our congregation. And even though these ministries still required schedules and systems, we found that those who took the time to participate in the experiences contained in the exercises at the end of this book were more concerned with living their faith across our church and community and were not just content to run with blinders on in their own compartmentalized ministry area.

When people are pursuing a way of living their faith that is personal to them, when they are investing themselves out of a sense of direction from the Holy Spirit, or are righting a wrong that deeply bothers them, they work harder and longer. We find they care more, it challenges them to grow more, and as they find to lead, they are more transformed. In the end, we found this sort of shared ownership of our church's ministries always resulted in a more invested team than if we handed attenders a schedule and told them to report to the homeless shelter to serve a meal every other Saturday from noon to 1:00.

The ministries that emerged also were more diverse and specialized than they would've been had the staff just sat in an office and decided to launch a set of programs. One young professional started a clothing donation and distribution system. Because she was a teacher, she was able to network within the schools and deliver the clothes to families who expressed need. Another woman revamped the church's existing financial assistance program, which sought to give support to families in financial crisis who could not afford basic necessities such as baby formula. A couple who did the training together became passionate about children in our community and executed the biggest Angel Tree effort I've ever witnessed. Another couple who owned a local garage had a vision for a single-parent car clinic that went on to offer oil changes and minor repairs to local moms and dads.

Another great bonus was that often when one attender would share about a personal passion for a specific kind of ministry, another attender would chime in that he or she also felt moved to do the same kind of work. Sometimes entire teams emerged as people discerned what God was doing in their consciences together. In addition, the people who spearheaded new initiatives were often so passionate about their respective ministries that their natural enthusiasm attracted other friends and acquaintances in the church to serve alongside them without us doing any recruiting.

Though I realize this approach to training may seem counterintuitive and even idealistic, let me reassure you: this arrangement did not leave us stranded or unable to fill posts in specific ministry areas. Rather, we saw a core group of attenders surface who had big-picture eyes. They often moved between programs and projects, seeing each as an opportunity to deepen the church's overarching commitment to love our community well.

But, what if? What if we would've found that none of our attenders were interested in volunteering in a certain program, say, providing Saturday day care so single moms could run errands? We determined we would pray about whether the lack of interest and passion toward this particular cause might be a sign we should pause or fold the declining ministry and put more attention on the areas where enthusiasm seemed strongest.

Summary: *Rather than training toward a specific agenda, allow attenders to own the dreaming process with you.*

Why This Type of Training

In search of some way to widen our concept of going, I eventually was driven back to reviewing my own experiences.

What about me had changed along the way? And what had caused this change? I wondered.

How had my life radically shifted, from viewing church as something I attended to viewing church as something I *am?* How had I shed my impression that God preferred to prance about brick and mortar establishments and begun looking for evidence of God's presence in the space between apartment buildings, city benches, and streetlights? How had I started to see hot dog vendors, wandering packs of teenagers, businesspeople lunching downtown, and weary moms standing in welfare lines as "belonging" to our local suburban church's mission just as much as the rows of people who passed the offering plate in its auditorium each Sunday?

As I reflected on the events which had slow-dripped a more portable version of faith into my veins—my childhood set in the intently focused home of a pastor and church planter, the four-year window spent soaking up a spiritual education both in and out of a Methodist college classroom—I could identify a long list of influences that had prodded my life in a going direction.

But most of the transformation had been sparked by experiences.

Experiences could be varied, of course. Some experiences were nothing more than fleeting but memory-charged moments, such as when a hungry man with soul-less eyes broke into suburbia and asked for a free sandwich at the small-town diner where I waitressed as a teenager. Others were more lengthy and planned, such as a trip to hand-pour concrete floors in the blanching sun of a Mexican border town.

Oftentimes, the experience was more formalized. For example, I noted—as many of you have no doubt observed as well—that mission trips and relief work often provided a tangible boost of new learning for myself and others.

There are few things more awkward or precious than listening to a person fresh off a plane from a service trip to a developing country. Theirs is a fumbling, divine feat as they furiously search the American vocabulary for words to communicate their experience.

The fact that missions team members have been changed is obvious. They are glowing like expectant mothers, their faces alive with animation, their hands nearly flying off their bodies as they describe all the towns and people and need they've just left.

These returnees grimace at the photos they snapped on their digital phones, having previously hoped that the hard lines etched into the face of the beggar they met outside a foreign city dump would grip you with the same ferocity that had changed them. But they can tell immediately that the story has lost something in the five-thousand-mile journey across the sea, that even as they draw from every sound effect and gesture their Western lives equipped them with, you do not see what they saw.

You cannot hear what they heard.

You do not feel what they felt.

What follows is a holy dissatisfaction, a frustrated urge to tell and show that cannot be satisfied by ordinary communication. They cannot convey how thick the grease was in the old man's hair, how they marveled at the magnificence of his trash-cobbled hut, or how simple joy collected itself in a mouth full of his cracked, decaying teeth.

And more frustratingly, they cannot convey to you *what it all meant.* How the experience rubbed up against their eighteen or forty-seven years of living in Illinois or Tennessee, how it left their understanding of sickness or social class in shambles, how it looped through their ideas about faith and hope and economic structures to teach them something they never quite grabbed hold of in their cinema-going or Super Bowl parties or intro to sociology class.

These mission team members are *awake,* consumed with purpose, energized by new perspective, and cued to how God might be prompting them to respond to the world they were born into.

And in the coming weeks, as they settle back into the old, familiar routines, this collision of information and experience often leads to massive increases in attentiveness.

The first days and weeks back on their home turf become days of sifting. They must add new perspective to old, stir home and mission site together, all the while skimming obsolete information and distractions off the top of their lives. They must compare, contrast, weigh *now* against *then*, *here* against *there*, continuously re-anchoring priorities with each reshuffling.

The regularity of reactions such as this was undeniable. The simple combination of new information and experience, followed by attentiveness, had grown my life and the lives of my friends case after case, time after time. And while the movement of the Holy Spirit can never be reduced to a formula, a seemingly reliable principle seemed to reveal itself.

If you consciously pause how you normally experience life—changing up the setting, the people, the tasks—and intentionally fix your mind on letting God immerse you in new learning, it tends to induce life change.

The challenge for a church, then, rests in how to expose large groups of people to such experiences.

To begin with, in most settings, only a handful of people pursued these sorts of experiences. In my case, in a congregation of one thousand, my mind quickly tried to calculate how many people had even been out of the country on more than a pleasure cruise? The number was small. And even if more people could be convinced of the value of a mission or relief trip, would their stage and position in life allow time and space for it?

There were certainly exceptions, but the great majority of people I knew who had undertaken mission and relief trips did so in their teens or twenties, before they were married, before they settled into jobs, before they reproduced short ones to leave Cheerios in the crevices of their couches and cars. But although some could no doubt be inspired to undertake trips later in life, it was unrealistic to think

79

every person could afford the impulse or the time or the finances to pour themselves into something so unconventional.

While thinking about our church's relationship with our community, I was a little disappointed we wouldn't be able to cart everyone to the plains of South Africa. And I was further saddened that I wouldn't even be able to get people to live two semesters in a homeless shelter in Chicago, as I did.

I wouldn't be able to derail four years of their lives into taking classes with fascinating names like "Social Stratification" or "Spirituality, Faith and Justice." I wouldn't be able to line their home libraries with titles like *God's Politics* or *Rich Christians in an Age of Hunger.* I wouldn't be able to introduce them to the specific, mostly urban people whose personalities, hearts, and stories had penetrated mine.

While at first I was disappointed that it wouldn't be possible to reproduce the circumstances that had inspired a more going faith in my life and in the lives of my friends, it of course quickly occurred to me that *maybe we didn't have to.*

After all, when Jesus spoke the word "going" to his disciples, they were required to get immunizations, apply for passports, and board planes to overseas locations. It hadn't even required coming up with Greyhound or Amtrak fare or booking an economy car at Enterprise. No, *going* was about wherever their feet took them. It was the ordinary town they'd grown up in, the lakes they'd fished a million times, that yawn of a hillside that had crouched in the background their whole lives.

The magic wasn't in the going . . . *far.*

It was in the spirit—or, some might say, the *obedience*—of going.

And the *going*—even the local going, the getting-about-the-public-sphere going—*did* seem to change the disciples.

It got them out of their holes and out of their siloed ways of looking at things. They trod beside those they probably would not have met otherwise—the Bethsaidan fishermen and the Canaanite zealot walking alongside the tax collector or physician. They met public officials, the paralyzed, the widowed, the possessed. And surely each of those stories changed them.

Transformation seemed more linked to how and *why* they went, not where or how far they went. And I could imagine growth occurred because of their intentionality as they prepped to go, because of the conversations that surfaced while going, and because of the learnings that resulted when they returned.

In fact, one might even argue that the disciples' method of going is preferable to the rarity and romance of a mission trip. Certainly one's local sphere is more accessible, more practical. But also perhaps more poignant. If we could introduce information and encourage experiences to inspire church people to be more attentive to the world they *really* live in on every ordinary day, one might argue the outcome, the level of daily impact on their surroundings, would be far more lasting and powerful.

Because our communities are the part of the world we were born into.

The ones we will wake up and walk into every day.

Where we already speak the language.

Where we will love people, work, perhaps get married and have children, grow old, and die.

These are the places we will go to over and over again, whether we carry faith with us or not.

It was out of these reflections that I began to develop the orientation ideas that follow.

These exercises are not designed to be linear. They don't ask people to memorize certain information or learn certain skills. Instead, these exercises expose people to new information, invite them to have new experiences that raise awareness and empathy and guide them in reflection on how they might respond.

Along these lines, each exercise presents one main idea— some act you can do with a group or, if you read the adaptation

81

suggestions, that you can adapt to do by yourself. And each comes with suggestions for discussing or reflecting on the activity.

Because the orientation exercises aim at personal growth and awareness, the activities provide just enough information to guide the reader through the experience and prompt reflection without giving them an "answer key." Because each person's growth is personal to them and because God moves in different ways, the "right answer" has less to do with coming up with a predetermined black-and-white fact and more to do with opening one's heart wider. Often the end goal of an exercise is not to come to a consensus but to discipline ourselves to hear varied perspectives from others who might look at the information or situation differently.

The exercises span a variety of activities. Some are focused on prayer and contemplation, some center on Bible study, some call for observation, and some require physical action. When facilitating orientations, group leaders should choose exercises or combinations of exercises that fit the time available and the group that is gathered. Some people may conduct all-day training sessions, in which groups do five or six of these exercises, moving from one to the next all in one day. Some may do an hour meeting each week in which they focus on just one or two activities.

How you choose and combine exercises is entirely up to you; however, you might benefit from beginning with activities that are focused on prayer or Bible study to set the stage. And you may also be well served by starting with activities that you feel attenders will be comfortable with, then gradually moving toward those you believe might be more challenging.

Finally, before you flip through the exercises or begin implementing them, I'll leave you with two suggestions. One, you may find it helpful to get a journal and devote it to your learnings about building relationship in the community. Write in it each time you do an exercise. And encourage group members who complete an exercise to get a copy of *Portable Faith* and do the remaining exercises by themselves, while journaling their learnings about each of them.

My second observation is that as you are exposed to this information and these new experiences, you may be tempted to feel defensive as your own ideas or perspectives are occasionally challenged. That's natural. My encouragement to you in these moments is to pause and reflect on why you feel defensive. What are you defending? Your own opinion? Your comfort? Your way of life? What are you afraid of losing? Human tradition? The truth of Scripture? The intentions of God? Invite God into personal reflection as you process your own internal responses. And you may want to journal these reservations or frustrations as well, as your own emotional triggers and intellectual responses may end up being just as revealing as the exercises themselves.

Exercises for the Portable Church

Exercise 1: Praying for Your Community
Prep Work Required: Approx. 30 minutes
Cost of Activity: Approx. $5.00 or less
Length of Time: 5 to 60 minutes

Materials

- recent editions of your local newspaper
- specific sections removed from your local phone book (suggestions: child care facilities, churches, care homes, government offices, hospitals, nonprofit organizations, parks, physicians, schools, senior citizen residences, and so on)
- photos or video footage of your city and/or its residents
- directories of local school staffs, fire department personnel, members of the military, and so on, printed from directories or websites
- calendars of community events printed from the local visitors' bureau or city website
- any literature or memorabilia that represent industries (automobile, for example) on which your community depends

Instructions

1. Create several table-based stations to display the images, information, and memorabilia related to your surrounding community. These items will serve as inspiration to pray for various parts of your town or city. You may do this by yourself, in a group, or in a congregational setting.

   To present the information in an appealing way, you might consider using tablecloths, framing certain photos, or placing literature in folders.

2. Mark off a specified amount of time for participants to visit the stations, gather information about your community, and return to their seats or another designated area to pray for your community.

   You may want to arrange for music to be played softly in the background to help participants ease smoothly into reflection.

3. Let your mind and God's spirit direct your thinking as you pray. You do not, for example, need to pray through a phonebook list *A* to *Z*, but as you scan the material, certain headlines or images may bring to mind certain people, groups, or issues that prompt prayer. For example, you may see a list of hospitals on a phonebook page and be reminded of the people in real time who are hurting in a local hospital as well as the local hospital staff trying to serve them.

4. Invite participants to take their newspaper page or other resource home and use it as a reminder to pray throughout the week. Also suggest that in the future, when they look at a phonebook or a newspaper, the visual can be a reminder to immerse themselves in community.

   Group size adaptations: If you are attempting this exercise alone, you might focus on just one reminder of the community—the newspaper or the phonebook, for example. Spend time praying over them, and then leave that item out in the open in your house for a week. Every time you see it, allow it to remind you of your desire to see church as a gathering of people to be sent rather than just a building.

Exercise 2: What God Has Done
Prep Work Required: 5 minutes to 5 hours
Cost of Activity: $1 each
Length of Time: 5 minutes to 60 minutes

Materials

- stones (decorative or driveway gravel, it doesn't matter)—at least 1 per person
- a roll of butcher paper, masking tape, and markers

or

- a county map for each participant or family

Instructions

1. Create a large map of your city or county using strips of butcher paper, taped together to form a large paper square. Using a map of your region, pencil in all major highways and roads. Once you have prepared the map, darken the lines with a marker, and add significant buildings. For example, you might want to label the location of your church building; city hall; local elementary, middle, and high schools; and so on.

2. Lay out the map in the room where your group will gather. Read or invite someone to read Joshua 4:1-7:

   When the whole nation had finished crossing the Jordan, the LORD said to Joshua, "Choose twelve men from among the people, one from each tribe, and tell them to take up twelve stones from the middle of the Jordan, from right where the priests are standing, and carry them over with you and put them down at the place where you stay tonight."

So Joshua called together the twelve men he had appointed from the Israelites, one from each tribe, and said to them, "Go over before the ark of the LORD your God into the middle of the Jordan. Each of you is to take up a stone on his shoulder, according to the number of the tribes of the Israelites, to serve as a sign among you. In the future, when your children ask you, 'What do these stones mean?' tell them that the flow of the Jordan was cut off before the ark of the covenant of the LORD. When it crossed the Jordan, the waters of the Jordan were cut off. These stones are to be a memorial to the people of Israel forever."

3. Although the Bible doesn't prescribe the act of placing rocks about one's environment or imply that this will bring a special blessing, it does repeatedly encourage the practice of remembering. Take the time to remember and tell as seen in Joshua 4. Invite those present to spend a few minutes in reflection while looking at the map with a spirit of gratitude for the community in which they live. Then, just as Israel set up a stone monument to mark the place where God did something among them, invite each person to place a stone on the map in a particular place where he or she felt God's presence in the community, experienced spiritual growth, or had a positive experience with other community members. Depending on the comfort level of the group, participants may share their monument by writing it on a card, talking about it in a conversation with just one other person or group, or revealing it to the entire gathering.

4. After Israel's experience at the Jordan, God unfolded a plan that would finally take them to the Promised Land they'd been anticipating for a generation. Two chapters later, for example, Joshua instructed the people of Israel to begin

marching around the city of Jericho, the first city west of the Jordan to be conquered by the Israelites as they advanced toward the Promised Land. In chapter 6, Joshua told the people, "Shout! For the LORD has given you the city! The city and all that is in it are to be devoted to the LORD" (vv. 16-17).

Most modern Western followers of God hold less militant roles than those of ancient Israel. Again, although not prescribed, the idea of physically walking around the land that God has provided for us and the notion of dedicating that geographic space to God are appropriate for people in any time and place.

Spend the next few minutes praying for the needs of your community as well as expressing anticipation for what God wants to do there in the future. Invite participants to stand up and walk over to various portions of the large map to pray for specific homes, places, or people that come to mind, if they wish. Also, encourage them, as people who express allegiance to God, to similarly invite God to be active in their region and pray for their own ability to sense where he is working.

Group size adaptations: In individual settings or in large congregations where it would be difficult to create a map large enough to accommodate this exercise, individual copies of city or county maps could be used. In this case, you might invite individuals or groups to draw symbols on their maps to represent their homes, the location of the church (if they attend), and other significant community buildings. They can also be encouraged to mark the location of something God did in the community in a different way, be it with a marker, stickers, or other materials. Rather than walk over the area for which they pray, they might physically place a hand or finger on that region. Again, placing a hand on a region is not a prescribed exercise that magically brings God's favor to that region; it is a reminder for those who pray to remember that God impacts the physical space in which we live.

Exercise 3: Reimagining Church
Prep Work Required: None
Cost of Activity: $0
Length of Time: 5 to 30 minutes

Materials

- a copy of *Portable Faith*

Instructions

1. Read the following "newspaper" story. One person can read aloud, or everyone can read silently.

Church Loses Building in Fire, Forced to Make Faith Portable

<Insert name of your city>—<Insert name of your church> was irreparably damaged by fire Thursday afternoon. Now, it seems, the congregation's insurance company will send in bulldozers and wrecking cranes to remove what is left of the walls and cart away the debris.

Over the past 48 hours, congregation members have been slowly stopping by the property to survey the damage and say good-bye to the building that has served them for <insert number> years.

Pastor <insert your pastor's last name> reported <he or she> and the church's board met yesterday evening to plan the church's next steps.

"It's going to take quite some time to rebuild the building. We estimate it will be at least a year before we can return to a structure on this property," the pastor acknowledged. "But this doesn't mean the church will stop operating. After all, the church is not the building. The church is the people."

The next steps for this church, he says, may not be what you'd expect.

According to this longtime pastor, the board will hold a town hall meeting where they will issue an unconventional challenge to their church's regular attenders.

"We could rent a facility and move our services to another site, but instead we're going to take a year off. We'll wait a full year before we draw up building designs or even break ground. And in that year, we're going to ask our congregation to submit ideas for how we could live and be church in the community without a regular meeting place."

The church's leaders say they will ask attenders to brainstorm how they could continue to serve all its previous purposes without a permanent location. "How can we commit to learning and worshiping? How can we serve the children of our community? How can we develop supportive networks of relationships for our attenders?"

Church members are asked to bring these ideas to the middle school at 7:00 p.m. this Friday.

"We plan on letting this tragedy become inspiration for reinvention," the pastor said resolutely. "After a year of living a more portable faith in this community, we may determine to build a different kind of building, one that is friendlier to community interaction. Or perhaps we will decide we don't even need a permanent building. Everything is up for grabs. Rather than invest our emotional energy into grieving our losses for a year, we're going to spend that year getting excited about what new things God might want to do in our church community."

2. Discuss the following:

- Imagine that this scenario actually unfolded for your church. How would you feel as the pastor announced this challenge?

- What would be the disadvantages of taking a year off from meeting in a permanent building? What would be the advantages?

- Would the prospect of reinventing church in this way disturb you or excite you? Why?

- Do you think, with prayer and reflection, you might arrive at a church model that carries out biblical ideas even more effectively? That serves the community even more? Why or why not?

3. Imagine the pastor and board asked you to present one of your ideas for how the congregation could express its faith without a building over the coming year. What is one idea you might suggest?

4. Discuss the idea among your group.

   Group size adaptations: If you are participating in this activity by yourself, you may want to record your answers to the questions then brainstorm any ideas in your journal.

Exercise 4: Impressions and Assumptions
Prep Work Required: 5 minutes
Cost of Activity: $0
Length of Time: 5 to 20 minutes

Materials

- a copy of *Portable Faith*

Instructions

1. This exercise is designed to help us think about our church building and systems from the perspective of a newcomer. Its intention is not to look for flaws in the church but to raise our awareness regarding obstacles or confusion a visitor might experience. Although we can't be sure what a guest

would think while visiting a weekend service for the first time, the practice of trying to put ourselves in the guest's shoes grows our awareness and reminds us that not everyone sees and experiences church the same way we do.

Either by yourself or in a small group, imagine you are a visitor coming to your church (or a church you previously attended) for the first time. Journal or discuss the impressions you believe visitors might have as they approach the building, walk around inside, attend a service, and so forth. Using the list below, think about each interaction attenders might have as they visit the church building, and try to identify any assumptions (correct or incorrect) they might make based on what they see and hear. Try to think of the various ways people could interpret what they experience, both positively and negatively. Write these down.

Example:

Observation: Everyone seems very busy.
Assumption: People must not want to talk to me!

Observation: Everyone seems very busy.
Assumption: People must really value this community to invest so much energy in it!

Note observations and assumptions guests might make as they approach the building from the road. *(Think about what they might see, including the building, the church property, signage, cars in the parking lot, and people wandering around.)*

Note observations and assumptions guests might make as they enter the building. *(Think about the general atmosphere in the foyer or lobby, the information table, the hospitality or snack area, as well as the people who might speak to them.)*

Note observations and assumptions guests might make as they drop their kids off. *(Think about the facilities or general atmosphere of the kids' ministry or nursery, as well as the volunteers who might interact with them.)*

Note observations and assumptions guests might make as they walk into the auditorium. *(Think about the general décor, the setup, the energy in the room, the crowdedness vs. availability of space, the lighting, the stage, and so on.)*

Note observations and assumptions guests might make during the service. *(Think about the program elements—sermon, video clips, announcements, songs, drama, offering, and any "insider language" used.)*

Note observations and assumptions guests might make as they leave. *(Think about the feel of the post-service auditorium and lobby. Are people rushing? Is anyone likely to ask how they enjoyed the service? To welcome them back the next week? To tell them about extracurricular church gatherings?)*

Note observations and assumptions guests might make as they attend a small group. *(Think about the neighborhood and house they might visit, the background of the people they would encounter, and so on.)*

2. Review the observations and assumptions you listed, and ask the following questions of each situation:

   • Could a visitor observing this situation misunderstand what he or she experiences in a way that hurts God's or the church's intentions? Why or why not?

   • What, if anything, could be done differently to avoid misperceptions?

   Group size adaptations: If you are doing this exercise alone, you might choose to journal your answers. If you are participating in a group, it might be helpful to post some photos of your church or a site map to encourage ideas to flow.

Exercise 5: The *All* in All People
Prep Work Required: 5 minutes
Cost of Activity: $0
Length of Time: 30 to 60 minutes

Materials

- a copy of *Portable Faith*
- a Bible

Instructions

1. Flip through the Gospels (Matthew, Mark, Luke, and John) in your Bible. Spend time reading subheadings for each chapter or section and scanning stories. As you browse, make a list of all the kinds of people with whom Jesus interacted. Examples might include a Samaritan woman, a blind man, and a rich young ruler. Make the list as extensive as possible.

2. Now work together to make a list of all the different types of people whom Jesus might encounter if he roamed within a ten-mile radius of your building. It may help you build your list to request that someone bring up city demographics from your city's website or from census.gov on a smart phone or a computer. It may also help to visualize the different parts of town and different kinds of buildings and what people he'd be likely to find in each. Think as broadly as possible. Examples might include factory workers, skaters, and immigrants.

3. Discuss the following statements as they relate to the identified groups, and decide whether the statement holds true or false for each particular group:

   ____ I am likely to interact with this person in passing, without any discomfort.

____ I could pursue friendship with this person and maintain it, allowing our families to intermix.

____ I could actively welcome this person into our church community.

____ I could learn from this person or serve on a team or ministry led by him or her.

Also, try to name stereotypes that you or others might hold about each group.

4. On the list you've made, circle any groups that, in your opinion, are unlikely to come to your church.

Discuss the circled groups using the following questions:

- Do you have any ideas about why they might not come?
- Do you think they are likely to interact with many attenders during the week?
- Are they likely to be invited? Why or why not?
- How might your church interact with or build relationships with these groups?

Group size adaptations: If you're working in a small group, you may want to split up the Gospels, assigning one person to browse through Matthew and another to flip through Mark and so on. Then have them share their findings. If you're working in a large group, you may want to divide the group into several smaller groups. Give each group one of the Gospel books. Groups may want to further divide the book by assigning groups of chapters to each person. One person looks through chapters 1–8, while another scans through 9–20, and so on. If you're working as an individual, you may want to give yourself several days to complete the assignment across several sittings, using your journal to make a list and to respond to the corresponding questions.

Exercise 6: Jesus' Table
Prep Work Required: None
Cost of Activity: $0
Length of Time: 60 to 90 minutes

Materials

- a copy of *Portable Faith*
- a Bible

Instructions

1. Look up the following passages. For each passage, write a one-sentence summary about what is happening or what idea is being presented. Also, record who (person or people) is involved in each story or passage.

Passage Collection #1

	One-Sentence Summary	People Mentioned
• Matthew 9:9-12:		
• Mark 6:30-44:		
• Luke 22:14-20:		
• Acts 2:		

- Luke 8:5-13:
- Acts 2:42-47:
- Luke 14:1-14:
- Matthew 25:35-40:

Passage Collection #2

	One-Sentence Summary	People Mentioned
John 6:48-58:		
John 4:17-28, 39-42:		
John 4:29-34:		
John 21:15-17:		
John 6:25-40:		

2. In the first set of passages, what common threads did you find?

3. In Luke 14, Jesus told his followers that they would be blessed if they invited people who were poor, disabled, and blind to their feasts. Several of these other passages show Jesus doing just that. Yet, many times this instruction to eat with the vulnerable doesn't seem to receive as much emphasis as other kinds of instruction in church tradition. Why do you think that might be?

4. Make a list of everyone you've eaten with in the last couple of months, and in parentheses, note where you ate. What patterns do you see in your eating habits? Do your mealtime companions look at all like Jesus' companions? Why or why not?

5. What changes could someone who does not interact with society's poor or marginalized persons make to ensure she or he would eat with a more diverse representation of your community? Try to think of examples that are especially practical and outrageously idealistic.

6. In the first set of passages, the Bible describes how those who followed God ate together and with members of the community. The second set of passages uses food as a metaphor, however. What is food a metaphor for?

7. Which seems more important to Jesus? The literal food or the metaphorical food? Why?

8. Do you believe the two practices—eating with people literally and offering them spiritual food—were connected for Jesus and his followers? In what ways did they go hand in hand?

9. Are the two practices connected for modern followers of Christ? And what implications does that have for churches in determining how to offer spiritual food to their communities?

10. Where, if at all, do you find eating together practiced in the church?

Group size adaptations: Individuals engaging in this activity alone may choose to answer these questions in their journals.

Exercise 7: Multiple Examples
Prep Work Required: None
Cost of Activity: $0
Length of Time: 5 to 20 minutes

Materials

- a copy of *Portable Faith*

Instructions

1. Read the following story to yourself, or ask someone to read it aloud:

> *It was a Sunday and the second morning worship service was in progress. One of the church staff members who had attended the church's early service was straightening the multiple stacks of brochures on the information table when she noticed a teary-eyed woman seemingly fleeing the auditorium.*
>
> *"Are you okay?" the staff person asked.*
>
> *The woman nodded, her cheeks flushing with apparent embarrassment at being caught displaying such obvious emotion.*
>
> *"Did something in the service impact you?" the staffer guessed, imagining that some scripture or insight had convicted or moved the woman.*
>
> *The woman nodded again and added, "But not in the way I'd hoped."*
>
> *The staffer pulled a few lobby chairs aside and invited the woman to sit down.*
>
> *"It's been a hard few months," the woman explained. "I had been a stay-at-home mom until my husband walked out on the kids and me in January. Since then, I've been working insane hours trying to keep my family together and make enough money to make ends meet. I even had to go on financial assistance, which I swore I'd never do. But with day care costs and hardly any child support coming in, I don't have a lot of options."*
>
> *"So it's been a bad year so far?" the staff person reflected, at first taking the woman's tears to be the sign of general frustration.*
>
> *"And a bad day today. Sorry, my nerves are frazzled. Today's message just scratched at the most vulnerable areas of my life."*
>
> *The staff person nodded, her mind racing through the sermon she'd heard in the earlier service, trying to guess how the*

woman's story connected to the topic. "Oh, the message is on tithing today, isn't it?" the staffer said compassionately. "That's gotta be tough to hear when money is so tight."

"It's not that," the woman replied. "It's the way the pastor was saying it. He kept saying we could all give a little extra to the building program if we just skipped that morning cup of Starbucks or went out to dinner one less time per week. Or if we bought one less new shirt or skipped the premium car wash and waxed our car ourselves."

The staffer swallowed hard, understanding dawning as the woman continued.

"He kept saying 'we' and 'us,' like all of us have this extra cash on hand for all these luxury items. But I haven't been able to afford a Starbucks coffee or to eat out or buy new clothes in months." The woman admitted, "As he was saying that, I was looking around at everyone else—women with their hair highlighted and nails professionally done, carrying name-brand purses, men with trendy shirts and designer glasses with expensive gadgets in their hands, and I started to feel like an outsider. Like I didn't belong here."

When they teach, pastors, leaders, and speakers naturally use examples from their lives. This is certainly appropriate because often our specific circumstances—having four children, traveling to Haiti, or being a champion pole vaulter in high school, for example—shape us and provide us with meaningful metaphors for understanding God and God's principles.

However, without ever intending to exclude, a leader's use of certain types of personal, social, class, or economic references can feel isolating to attenders who don't relate, particularly when the examples fit everyone except members of a minority group.

Although sometimes people misperceive our comments or take them personally because of their own hurt, for which we are not responsible, it is wise to take a few minutes when preparing examples to intentionally think about how the various groups who might be present would relate.

When we do this, we may find our lives provide an alternative example that connects with more people or avoids isolating others. Or we may be able to offer multiple examples in order to demonstrate that the principle we're sharing applies to many kinds of people, not just one kind.

2. Read the following statements that could be made by a pastor, a leader, or a teacher, and try to rewrite each one to make it connect with the most people. To do this, (a) try to think of an alternative example that is more universal, (b) try to think of additional examples that could make the statement apply more broadly, or (c) try to write a disclaimer that could demonstrate that the speaker is sensitive to people who do not relate.

For example, when speaking about determination, a church leader who was a successful high school athlete might say something like "We all know what it was like to work hard, running sprints day after day, but then to cross the line first in the hundred-yard dash . . ." To help more people relate well, even those who were cut from high school sports programs or never participated in them, the speaker could think of an alternative way of making the same point.

- **Broadening the example:** "Think of a goal you worked really hard at, and then try to remember what it felt like when you achieved that goal. Exhilarating, right?"
- **Including additional examples:** "Maybe you know what it's like to work hard, running sprints day after day as an athlete, practicing the same classical piece again and again as a musician, or trying to get everything done before the extended family shows up for Christmas dinner."

- **Demonstrating awareness and sensitivity:** "Now I know not everyone was obsessed with sports like I was, but the way this hits home for me is . . ."

Read the following examples. Record groups that might feel in some way excluded by or unable to relate to the statement. Rewrite the following examples in a way that would come across as less isolating. If you think the example is bad enough, you might recommend cutting it altogether.

Once you get really good at it, you might purposefully start choosing examples that fit your audience. That was what Jesus did. Consider the following:

- "We all know what it's like to sit in that mortgage office and sign away our lives to purchase our dream home . . ."
- "Now, of course, around here we don't have to worry about crime."
- "Can you imagine getting into that much debt? What was that guy thinking?"
- "You know the thing that seemed like a good idea but ended up being a lot more trouble than you expected. Like our in-ground swimming pool . . ."
- "Sometimes I need quiet time. It's nice that so many church families invite me to dinner or to hang out with them, but sometimes—you know how it is—I just need alone time."
- "I don't know about you, but my kids have to have the Nikes."
- "It's like the day you find out you're getting a promotion."
- "I'm telling you, this homeless guy was used up. He was overweight, wearing three winter coats, smoking a pipe, and had a crazy lazy eye."
- "Fasting is like regular maintenance that keeps your spiritual life healthy. It's just like how every four weeks, my wife goes down to the salon and gets a highlight and a manicure

to keep her body looking good. Fasting keeps the soul looking good."

- "It's like when you save up to buy that first four-wheeler or
  Jet Ski or motor home."

Group size adaptations: None are necessary. This activity can be completed by an individual, a small group, or an
entire congregation. If you are doing this on your own, you
may want to record your responses in your journal.

Exercise 8: Role Change

Prep Work Required: None

Cost of Activity: $0

Length of Time: 30 to 60 minutes

Materials

- a Bible
- a copy of *Portable Faith*

Instructions

1. Most of us believe that the Bible was written to convey
   God's intended meaning, yet we may not always stop to
   think about how different people may respond differently
   to biblical passages. Of course, people can interpret a verse
   or larger section of Scripture differently from a theological perspective. In this case, I'm not talking about doctrinal differences as much as a person's way of identifying
   with Scripture.

   If you grew up in a middle-class, white congregation, for
   example, as I did, you might have naturally identified with

people or ideas in a story that people of another social or economic group may not relate to.

For example, when as a child I heard the story of the paralytic whose friends lowered him through the roof to see Jesus, I always envisioned myself as one of the people on the roof. I was not paralyzed, nor did I have any obvious physical challenge or sickness for which I would be seeking healing from Jesus. But I did believe Jesus could heal, and I could imagine myself going to extremes to help a friend gain access to Jesus.

You can imagine how surprised I was while attending an urban church in my early twenties, when the pastor preached the whole message from the perspective of the man who needed to be healed. It was clear that many in the congregation who experienced suffering and hardship, some of whom had ailments, were naturally drawn to this perspective. They could imagine themselves being lowered in front of the Savior by their friends.

Similarly, while I was attending worship at a homeless shelter, a speaker referenced the story in Mark 12:41-44 of the widow who gives her last copper coins. I had always imagined sitting in a pew and watching this woman go forward to put in her last coins, but the other attenders at the shelter imagined themselves as the woman!

Does it change the meaning? No. Yet for me, in the first case, I was viewing the story in a somewhat detached way, seeing myself as a middleman who felt appreciative of the way God healed those who needed it, but they were seeing Jesus as a *healer*, someone who could reach down and touch their broken bodies and heal *them*. And in the second case, I was projecting a sacrifice onto someone else, while the others felt they were being challenged to sacrifice their own wages or savings.

When we speak about a passage, it might be a good idea to remember we shouldn't assume that everyone in the audience easily relates to the same person we do.

2. Think about the following stories, and if necessary, look them up and read them. Consider which person you relate to most in each story. In addition, try to determine what in a person's background or circumstances might lead him or her to relate better to a different figure in the story.

- Jesus' birth (Matt. 2:1-12: Luke 2:1-21): wise men, shepherds, parents of Jesus, innkeeper

- John baptizing (Matt. 3:1-11): the baptizer, the person being baptized, the strict religious rulers watching

- Jesus healing demon-possessed people (Matt. 8:28-34): Jesus, the demon-possessed people, the herdsmen, the people of the town who begged Jesus to leave

- Jesus healing the paralytic (Matt. 9:1-8): Jesus, the paralytic, the friends of the paralytic, the crowd watching

- Jesus feeding the five thousand (Matt. 14:13-21): Jesus, the people who listened to him and became hungry, the disciples

- Jesus walking on the water (Matt. 14:22-33): Jesus, the disciples in the boat, Peter

- the parable of the lost sheep (Matt. 18:10-14): the shepherd, the lost sheep, one of the ninety-nine sheep safe in the flock

- the children coming to Jesus (Matt. 19:13-15): Jesus, the children, the children's parents, the disciples

- the rich young man (Matt. 19:16-30): Jesus, the rich young man, the disciples who were angry because it seemed impossible to get into heaven

- the laborers in the vineyard (Matt. 20:1-16): the foreman, the laborers who began work early, the laborers who came midday

- the parable of the two sons (Matt. 21:28-32): the father who owned the vineyard, the son who said he wouldn't work but did, the son who said he would work but didn't

- the parable of the talents (Matt. 25:14-30): the master, the servants who doubled their money, the servant who buried the money in the ground

- the parable of the prodigal son (Luke 15:11-32): the son who stayed, the son who left, the father

3. When you look back over the list and the people you identified with, how might the way you read the story and the learning you take from it differ if you had different life circumstances?

   Group size adaptations: Large groups could choose to highlight just a few of the bulleted Scripture passages with the whole group and then invite people to share which person they would relate to most. They could share this aloud to the entire group or, if the group is not comfortable with public expression, they could share responses with just one partner. Individuals may want to respond to each passage in their journals.

Exercise 9: How Jesus Showed Belonging
Prep Work Required: None
Cost of Activity: $0
Length of Time: 60 minutes

Materials

- a Bible
- a copy of *Portable Faith*

Instructions

1. As we try to live our faith in our communities, we invite people into not only a local gathering of believers but also a historic and global membership. How do we make them feel welcome in our local church (should they choose to visit or attend) and in our lives?

   How can they experience church while in the presence of those who follow God, in the words and actions exchanged between them?

   Read the passages below, looking for the way that Jesus invited people to belong via his actions, his stories, and his language when speaking to them. Summarize how Jesus invited belonging in each passage.

   Passage **How He Invited Belonging**

   Example, Matthew 8:1-4: Immediately after healing him, Jesus went out of his way to tell the man with leprosy to go to the priest so the priest could declare him clean and he could be reintroduced to society.

   Example, Matthew 8:5-13: Jesus told the Roman centurion, someone who would not necessarily have been viewed as a religious man, that he had not seen such faith in all of Israel. This was an affirming statement, given how Jesus had interacted with many religious officials and yet found the centurion's faith to be more evident.

- Matthew 9:9-13:
- Matthew 9:27-31:
- Matthew 12:46-50:
- Matthew 18:10-14:
- Matthew 19:13-15:
- Mark 5:21-34:
- Mark 10:46-52:
- Luke 15:8-10:
- Luke 15:11-32:
- Luke 17:11-19:

2. What does your church—or other modern-day churches—typically do to invite people to belong? Do you believe the typical church of today goes to the same lengths Jesus did or shows similar intentionality in trying to make everyone—including society's most judged or most vulnerable—belong? Why or why not?

3. Who are the hardest people in society for you to welcome? How do you think Jesus would interact with those people?

Group size adaptations: None are necessary. This activity can be completed by an individual, a small group, or an entire congregation. If you are completing this exercise on your own, write your responses in your journal.

Exercise 10: Jesus' Attitude toward Religion
Prep Work Required: None
Cost of Activity: $0
Length of Time: 60 minutes

Materials

- a Bible
- a copy of *Portable Faith*

Instructions

1. Many who had awaited the coming of Jesus expected him to set up an empire in which he would elevate the Jews to power. One might have expected Jesus to align himself with the most notable Jewish leaders of the time, fraternizing and building affinity with temple leaders or religious zealots. However, there seemed to be no group with whom Jesus was more at odds—whose tension spanned more verses—than the religious elite.

   Read the passages below, and summarize the interaction between Jesus and the religious leaders in one sentence.

   Religious Leaders   **Summary**

   Example, Matthew 9:1-8: Scribes criticized him for telling the paralytic his sins were forgiven.

   - Matthew 9:9-12:
   - Matthew 12:9-14:
   - Matthew 21:12-13:
   - Matthew 21:14-17:
   - Matthew 22:23-33:
   - Matthew 23:1-36:
   - Mark 2:18-28:
   - Mark 5:35-42:

- Mark 7:1-13:
- Mark 8:11-13:
- Mark 8:14-21:
- Mark 12:13-17:
- Mark 12:38-40:
- Luke 6:6-11:
- Luke 11:37-44:
- Luke 13:10-17:
- Luke 14:1-6:
- Luke 16:14-17:
- John 7:40-51:
- John 9:1-41:

2. What attitudes and beliefs might have encouraged the religious leaders to incite tension with Jesus?

3. The religious leaders criticized Jesus for spending time with unholy, irreligious people and for breaking the religious rules deemed important by their institution. Are these criticisms, in your opinion, ones often levied against religious leaders today? Why or why not?

4. In Matthew 23:1-36, Jesus expanded on how the religious leaders had gone wrong. He made the following observations:

- They did not practice what they claimed to believe.
- They made others' lives harder by burdening them (likely by their judgment and insistence on keeping religious rules), while living an easy life.
- They did good deeds to be noticed.
- They revered religious leaders in place of God.

- Their converts were hypocritical and judgmental.

- They neglected what Jesus called weightier matters of the law: justice and mercy and faithfulness.

- They put on a façade, appearing holy on the outside but indulging in sin on the inside.

- They did not recognize the messages/messengers God sent.

If Jesus were to come in this era, do you think he would find examples of these things in today's churches? If so, which ones do you think are most likely to sidetrack modern-day churches?

Group size adaptations: None are necessary. This activity can be completed by an individual, a small group, or an entire congregation. If you are completing this exercise on your own, write your responses in your journal.

Exercise 11: Grace
Prep Work Required: None
Cost of Activity: $0
Length of Time: 60 minutes

Materials

- a Bible
- a copy of *Portable Faith*

Instructions

1. The religious institutions of Jesus' day spent a lot of time determining who was right and wrong and identifying those

who broke religious law, but Jesus never seemed willing to enforce their judgment or affirm their superiority.

Read the following passages, and summarize how Jesus' words or actions encouraged grace and humility:

- Matthew 7:1-5:

- Matthew 7:12:

- Matthew 9:13:

- Matthew 18:1-4:

- Luke 7:36-50:

- John 8:1-11:

- John 13:1-20:

2. Jesus let several people—the sinful woman from the city (Luke 7), the Samaritan woman at the well (John 4), and the woman who committed adultery (John 8)—go without punishment or mistreatment (and with the admonition, at times, to sin no more). However, some who claim to follow Jesus, both in his time and in ours, are more likely to shame and judge those who've committed sins along these lines. Why might those who are religious—in Jesus' generation or in ours—be especially prone to judgment?

3. Jesus never seemed to harshly treat or exclude any sinner or outsider he encountered. While you search through the Gospels, who does Jesus seem to judge harshly?

4. In Matthew 9:13 the religious people of his day criticized Jesus for eating with sinners. One comment that he made in response was that he desired "mercy, not sacrifice." What do you think this means?

5. In modern-day society, when are you tempted to demand sacrifice over mercy? Try to think about when you may be prone to lay down grace and demand blood in regard to certain people or sins.

6. Which is heresy: to give someone grace that a religious leader or church doesn't think the person deserves, or to act as though a person's sin falls outside the grace of God?

   Group size adaptations: None are necessary. This activity can be completed by an individual, a small group, or an entire congregation.

Exercise 12: How Jesus Showed Belonging
Prep Work Required: None
Cost of Activity: $0
Length of Time: 60 minutes

Materials

- a Bible
- a copy of *Portable Faith*

Instructions

1. Ask participants to line up on an imaginary line. Read the following statements, and instruct people to move to the far right of the line if they agree with the statement or to the far left of the line if they disagree with it. If they are uncertain or think the statement could be partially true, they may choose a place somewhere in the middle. After people take their positions, pick two or three people and ask them why they chose to stand where they did. To keep the group comfortable, invite anyone who does not wish to further explain his or her position on the line to pass.

- If we keep more than we need, it is like stealing from those in need.

- If God gives us more than we need, God intends for us to pass it on to someone in need.

- Feasting is not a sin. Feasting on the world's riches in front of those who are starving is a sin.

- The more you own, the more time, energy, and money you must spend maintaining, protecting, and insuring what you own.

- The less you own, the less likely you are to be in debt, and the more ability you would have to bless others.

- Those who own less, and are less likely to be in debt, probably experience less personal pressure and more freedom.

- Society encourages us to own more or to upgrade what we own so that we never seem to achieve contentment.

- A very rich person might struggle more in coming to God than a poor one.

- Every person has the right to own as much as she or he wants.

2. Read the following passages. For each passage, summarize what the Bible says about money and possessions in one sentence:

- Matthew 19:16-30:
- Mark 12:1-7:
- Luke 16:14-17:
- Luke 16:19-31:
- Luke 18:18-30:

3. Which of these passages is the most difficult for you to relate to or put into practice?

4. Would someone who owned less perhaps be more prepared to pick up and "go" if God prompted her or him to do so?

Group size adaptations: None are necessary. This activity can be completed by an individual, a small group, or an entire congregation. If you are completing the exercise on your own, you may want to record your responses in your journal.

Exercise 13: Where Jesus Went

Prep Work Required: None

Cost of Activity: $0

Length of Time: 60 minutes

Materials

- a Bible
- a copy of *Portable Faith*

Instructions

1. Flip through the book of Matthew, starting with chapter 9 (or all four Gospels if you have a large group and can break it up), and record all of the places where Jesus went.

The places Jesus went in chapters 1–8 are already recorded:

Where Jesus Went

- a stable (where he was born)
- Egypt (where he was a refugee)
- Nazareth (where his family settled)
- the wilderness (where he was baptized and later tempted by the devil)
- Capernaum (where he went to live after his ministry began)
- the sea (where he recruited disciples as he walked beside it)
- throughout Galilee (where he taught and did miracles)
- the mountain (where the crowd followed him)

2. List all of the places you have gone in the last week.

   Examples: Work, the grocery store, the kids' soccer game

3. As you survey the list you made, does your current lifestyle include time going into the community?

4. Do you use the time you are in the community to intentionally build relationships and serve those in need, or do you end up in the public sphere for other agendas? What are those other agendas?

5. How could you use some of the time you already spend in the public sphere to serve the people of the community?

   Group size adaptations: None are necessary. This activity can be completed by an individual, a small group, or an entire congregation. If you are completing the exercise on your own, you may want to record your responses in your journal.

Exercise 14: Budget Your Money

Prep Work Required: 5 minutes

Cost of Activity: The cost of a Monopoly board game (if you cannot borrow it)

Length of Time: 60 minutes to 2 hours

Materials

- classified section of local newspaper or access to online version of local paper
- Monopoly game

Instructions

1. If you are doing this exercise with a large group, ask people to bring in their Monopoly games; and it would be helpful to have several boards. Set up a game of Monopoly in which the game is slightly altered. Play with normal rules, but distribute money, the listed properties, and houses/hotels at the start of the game:

Player 1:

Cash: $5,000

Properties: Boardwalk and Park Place, with one hotel each

Connecticut Ave., Vermont Ave., and Oriental Ave., with two houses each

Player 2:

Cash: $500

Properties: None

If there are additional players . . .

Player 3:

Cash: $1,500

Properties: None

Player 4:

Cash: $1,500

Properties: Baltic Avenue and Mediterranean Avenue, with one house each

Play the game according to normal rules for 15 minutes, then stop, unless someone wins before the 15-minute mark.

If there are more than four people, additional players should get the same allotment as Player 3.

2. When the 15 minutes are up, ask the group to discuss the following questions:

- How did you feel when you saw how much you started with or were "born" with? What did you feel about your chances of success?

- As the game progressed, was there ever a point where someone felt frustrated or helpless in game play? Why did that happen?

- Did anyone at the table display arrogance or gloat?

- Did anyone at the table feel guilty or apologetic? Why?

- Did anyone at the table cheat or consider cheating? Why?

- If your goal was to win, did the new rules make the game harder or easier?

- How might these experiences transfer to real life?

3. Imagine you are the head of a four-person household, and your income is $21,000 per year, or $1,750 per month. This amount is below the poverty line. Below, plan a monthly budget showing how you would spend your income, using standard prices estimated from the cost of living in your area:

- mortgage or rent:
- homeowner's or renter's insurance:
- property taxes:
- electricity:
- water:
- gas:
- phone:
- groceries:
- health insurance:
- car payment:
- car insurance:
- gasoline:
- other transportation (bus and so on):
- student loans:
- day care/babysitting:
- house repairs:
- entertainment:
- vacation:
- fitness:
- eating out:
- Internet:
- pets:

- clothing:
- savings:
- toiletries:
- household products:
- gifts:
- haircuts:
- cosmetics:

4. Discuss the following questions as a group:

   - Was it difficult for you to figure out how to create this budget in a way that made ends meet for your family?
   - Have you had experiences where you've had to penny-pinch that helped you decide how to distribute money? Or was budgeting for a small amount of money a new undertaking?
   - Were you satisfied that you could cover a family's basic needs with the amount of money you had to work with? Why or why not?
   - What items did you deem nonessential and decide to cut?
   - How many of the nonessential items that you cut do you or your family enjoy in real life?
   - Do you think you would experience any of the same frustrations that arose in the Monopoly game (but at a deeper level) if you or your children had to cut out some of these nonessential items?

5. Imagine you are told that because of your low income, you may be eligible for some sort of government assistance.

To find out whether you are eligible, you have to fill out an application for TANF (Temporary Assistance for Needy Families), http://singleparents.about.com/od/financialhelp/a/find_TANF.htm.

Look over the application closely, or take the time to fill it out based on your family's information.

Although every state's assistance programs are slightly different, if a family of four qualifies for government support, they can expect to receive Medicaid health benefits and about $432 a month in food vouchers. They would be ineligible for cash assistance. Go back and erase or cross out the amount you allotted for food, and redistribute it to other areas where you believe it is needed.

- In what areas did you decide to spend the $432? Were any of them nonessentials, such as entertainment? Or were you still just trying to make ends meet?

- Was the paperwork to apply for assistance straightforward, or was it difficult to understand? Are there portions you anticipate that someone with a low reading level might struggle to comprehend?

- If you were in this circumstance in real life and were told you could apply for benefits, do you think you would opt to do so? Why or why not?

- What kinds of feelings might you experience as you arrived at a welfare office to turn in this application?

- What kind of stigma do you feel could be associated with receiving benefits in your community?

6. As you look at the budget you've been working on, what kinds of things might an individual do to serve a family in need? (For example, babysit for free, or offer to trade babysitting services with them.)

What kinds of things might a church be able to do to serve a family in need? (For example, opening up the gym for free rec time.)

Group size adaptations: None are necessary. This activity can be completed by a small group or an entire congregation. If you are completing the exercise on your own, you will not be able to play the Monopoly portion, but you can respond to the questions in your journal. Perhaps the next time you play board games, if you occasionally do so, you could play this altered game of Monopoly.

Exercise 15: Watching for Learning
Prep Work Required: 5 to 30 minutes
Cost of Activity: $5 to $20
Length of Time: 2 to 3 hours

Materials

- the film you choose to rent
- a copy of *Portable Faith*

Instructions

1. Rent a movie or documentary focusing on a particular social group that might help you or the group examine how you interact with, judge, and sometimes detach from certain people groups.

    Please keep in mind that every denomination, church, or group of Christians may have different tastes and standards for watching movies. While the films below include only movies rated PG-13 or less or unrated documentaries and news reports, they may portray hardship by using language or other elements that could be offensive to some viewers. Please screen films to determine whether they are appropriate for your setting before showing them.

For those who enjoy films of this nature and who are comfortable with a wide range of movie genres and ratings, search the hundreds of movies online by using terms such as "sociology videos."

Some of these videos may be available online at no charge:

- *There Are No Children Here* (1993); made for TV/unrated; urban youth
- *Class Dismissed: How TV Frames the Working Class* (2005); documentary/unrated; working class
- *John Q.* (2002); PG-13; underinsured
- *Waiting for Superman* (2010); PG; undereducated
- *People Like Us: Social Class in America* (2001); made for TV/unrated; America's social classes
- *Freedom Writers* (2007); PG-13; urban youth
- *Finding Forrester* (2000); PG-13; urban youth, retired professional
- *Country Boys* (2002); made for TV/unrated; rural youth, undereducated, financially challenged
- *A Dream in Doubt* (2007); made for TV/unrated; immigrants, Sikhs
- *True Colors* (1991); made for TV/unrated; whites and blacks
- *Throwaway Teens* (1999); made for TV/unrated; gay teens kicked out by parents
- *Streetwatch* (1994); documentary; homeless and officials

A large number of similar clips are available at the following website: www.thesociologicalcinema.com/videos.html.

2. When you've finished watching the film, journal about or discuss the following questions. You may want to take notes during the movie.

- What people groups were portrayed in the film?

- What hardships or unique circumstances, if any, did these people face that you have experienced? Which have you not experienced?

- What kinds of emotional responses, if any, did you feel while watching their stories?

- If you felt any kinds of emotional reactions while watching, did this surprise you? Why or why not?

- Are these people groups found in your local community? And if so, how often—if at all—would you likely run into them? Under what circumstances?

- If the members of these groups were present in your local community, would they likely attend your church? Why or why not?

- If church attenders were to go to people like those portrayed in the film, where would they be likely to interact with them?

- Do these people groups have practical needs that a church in their area could support them in meeting? What are they, and how might people of faith help?

- If you were to integrate members of these people groups into your congregation, do you think existing attenders would struggle to interact with or accept them? Why or why not?

- Do you think any people groups shown in the film might take offense with how the movie portrays them?

Group size adaptations: None are necessary. This activity can be completed by an individual, a small group, or an entire congregation. If you are completing the exercise on your own, you may want to record your responses in your journal.

Exercise 16: How We Click
Prep Work Required: None
Cost of Activity: $0
Length of Time: 5 to 20 minutes

Materials

- a computer or other device with Internet access
- a copy of *Portable Faith*

Instructions

1. Take ten minutes to visit a few of your favorite news websites. While you are looking at the front page of the news site, study the titles of the stories without clicking on the links or reading the actual stories. On a separate sheet of paper, make a list of the titles you would likely read on a typical visit to the news site. Next to it, make a second column of the titles you might read, and add a third column of titles you would probably skip on a typical visit.

2. Review the titles in each column. Journal about or discuss the following:

- What types of stories are you most likely to click on? What do these stories have in common? Do they tend to be happy stories, serious stories, sad stories? Are they about politics? The economy? Sports?

- Next, take a look at the titles you'd be least likely to click on. What kinds of stories do you tend to skip?

- Are you more likely to click on stories about people you can relate to? People who have something in common with you? People who live near the part of the country where you grew up? People who have the same color skin and so on?

- Do you find it difficult to humanize stories about tragedy when they happen far away from where you live? Is it something you tend to shrug off because it doesn't have any personal impact?

3. Do you feel your news reading habits betray any personal biases? If so, which ones?

Group size adaptations: None are necessary. This activity can be completed by an individual, a small group, or an entire congregation. If you are completing the exercise on your own, you may want to record your responses in your journal.

Exercise 17: All People's Eyes
Prep Work Required: None
Cost of Activity: $0
Length of Time: 20 to 60 minutes

Materials

- a copy of *Portable Faith*

Instructions

1. Walk through the church building, especially the hallway and lobby area. Who do you think designed it? Do the color scheme, décor, and other features play to a certain race or social group? What symbols, artwork, images, or other features could be tastefully integrated into the design to convey a welcome to different people groups living in your city?

2. Sit through a service. What kinds of artwork or images are displayed on stage or on the big screen? Does the background of slides tend to be rural landscapes, or does it include urban settings or skylines? What about the music? Is there music from a variety of genres? Is there an attempt to include worship songs that might connect with multiple cultures represented in your city? What about the people onstage? Do they all look like they just stepped out of an Urban Outfitters or Gap catalog, or are a variety of styles represented?

3. Browse the literature on the church information table. Does it expressly state that all people are welcome? If it contains photos, are the photos of a variety of people who represent the demographics in your city or county, or does it present dozens of people who look like clones of each other?

4. What about the membership manual? Does the mission or vision statement include an emphasis on welcoming and building relationship with all people? Is the idea of portable faith, of being a going church, represented anywhere in the core values or doctrinal statements?

   Group size adaptations: None are necessary. This activity can be completed by an individual, a small group, or an entire congregation. If you are completing the exercise on your own, you may want to record your responses in your journal.

Exercise 18: Neighborhood Map
Prep Work Required: 5 minutes
Cost of Activity: None
Length of Time: 20 minutes

Materials

- a sheet of copy paper and a writing implement for each participant
- a copy of *Portable Faith*

Instructions

1. Draw a simple map of your neighborhood. Make sure to label your house as well as the houses of your neighbors. Label as many neighbors' homes as you can, and include the last names of the owners—if you know them—and the first names of all you can remember who live at each house.

2. Discuss the following:

   - What does your map include? Did you include any landmarks? Swing sets? Decks? Pools? How detailed is it? Did you include any public spaces like parks? If you didn't include these items, would you be able to do so if asked? Why or why not?

   - How far out did you draw from your house? What logic did you employ to determine how big an area to define as your neighborhood?

   - What lies beyond the area you drew? Could you go farther out, or do you not know the lay of the roads or the location of homes to draw?

   - After drawing your neighborhood, do you feel that you know your neighborhood well, or do you feel that you have only a very basic grasp of it? Explain your answer.

Group size adaptations: None are necessary. This activity can be completed by an individual, a small group, or an entire congregation. If you are completing the exercise on your own, you may want to record your responses in your journal.

Exercise 19: Map Your People
Prep Work Required: None
Cost of Activity: $2 to $10
Length of Time: 10 to 20 minutes

Materials

- a local map
- a church directory

Instructions

1. Post a large map on a bulletin board, or tape it to a whiteboard or easel in the room. Mark the location of your church building with a star. If you are unable to buy the map, you may be able to acquire one at no cost from your local tourism bureau or city government.

2. Ask each person in the room to go up to the map, one at a time, and draw dots on the following places: home, workplace, school that a family member attends in the community, and additional buildings or gathering spots—besides gas stations, stores—where the person goes on a weekly basis (such as a gymnasium, a library, or a park). Then before the person sits down, ask her or him to draw a line between (a) home and church; (b) home and workplace; (c) home and school; and (d) home and other frequented buildings.

3. When everyone has finished, look at the map together, and analyze what you see.

- Are all of the lines on the same side of town, or are they spread out?
- Are sections of the map entirely untouched by lines, indicating that attenders do not frequent them?
- What are basic ways to influence untouched areas of the city?

Options might include

A. building relationships in that part of the community so that new people from that area become part of what you're doing;

B. sending attenders to relocate to the untouched areas of the community;

C. finding ways of living church in that part of the community, regardless of whether attenders ever come to the actual church building.

Group size adaptations: If you are completing the exercise on your own, you may want to use the church directory and plot the houses of all listed members on the map. Then answer the discussion questions in your journal.

Exercise 20: Bead Community
Prep Work Required: 30 minutes
Cost of Activity: $10
Length of Time: 10 to 30 minutes

Materials

- a printout of the census data for your community: Go to http://factfinder2.census.gov. In the quick start search area on the front page, type "income" in the topic box, and in the place box, type the name of your city or county. Print results. Go back to the homepage. In the topic area type "race," and in the place box, type the name of your county or city. Print results.
- one small clear plastic cup or plastic zippered bag for each participant
- one paper or plastic bowl or container for each color bead.
- one clear bowl or container (plastic or glass), the size of a cereal or salad bowl or larger
- large plastic craft beads, most typically used for children's bracelets

There are two activities. For the first one you will need the following colored beads:

- yellow for upper class
- green for middle class
- red for people in financial need

For the second activity, you will need the following colors:

- blue for European descent
- red for African descent
- green for South American descent
- purple for Asian descent
- orange for Middle Eastern descent
- yellow for Australian descent

Instructions

1. Pour the beads into the bowls/containers, using one color per container, and set them in the middle of a table surrounded by chairs.

2. Place a clear plastic cup or plastic zippered bag at each seat.

3. Post a list of bead colors along with the people groups that each represents.

4. Activity 1: Invite a host to read the questions below, one at a time. Using only the yellow, green, and red beads, have participants answer each question by taking the appropriate beads out of the center bowls and placing them in their cups or bags.

   When you're finished with the questions, instruct participants to look at their cups and reflect on the socioeconomic diversity in their lives. Then pour all the cups into the large clear bowl, and look at the network of relationships represented by the entire group.

   Compare the general diversity represented in the bowl to the general makeup of your city/county represented in the census data. Do the participants interact with all groups in your city? Are any missing? If everyone in your group attends the same church, is there a similar proportion of diversity in the bowl as there is in your city/county?

5. Activity 2: Invite a host to read the questions below one at a time. Using all the beads, have participants answer each question by taking the appropriate beads out of the center bowls and placing them in their cups or bags.

   When you're finished with the questions, instruct participants to look at their cups and reflect on the cultural diversity in their lives. Then pour the contents of all the cups into the large clear bowl, and look at the network of relationships represented by the entire group.

Questions

- Which people groups live on either side of your house?

- Which groups live in your neighborhood?

- Which groups represent the people you work with? (If you work in a large company, just think of your department.)

- Which groups are in your immediate family? (Include your parents and siblings if you live at home with your parents; include your spouse and children if you have moved out of your house and are married; include only yourself if you are single.)

- Which groups are in your extended family? (Include your current household, your parents, your siblings, your in-laws, your nephews and nieces, your parents' siblings, and your first cousins.)

- Which groups attend your child's school (or the district where you live)?

- Which groups represent the two friends with whom you spend the most time?

6. Journal about or discuss the following reflection questions:

- Was there a lot of diversity in your life?

- Were you surprised by either the diversity or the lack of diversity reflected in your cup? Why or why not?

- Were you surprised by either the diversity or the lack of diversity reflected in the group bowl? Why or why not?

- Was there a majority socioeconomic group/cultural group represented in your cup? What is it? Why do you think that is?

- Was there a majority socioeconomic group/cultural group represented in your bowl? What is it? Why do you think that is? Is it okay, in your opinion, for a church to serve mostly one socioeconomic group/cultural group?

- What are the advantages and disadvantages of a church that serves only one primary socioeconomic group or cultural group?

- People of faith don't aim at diversity for diversity's sake. What might be good reasons—theological, logical, or other—to try to build relationships with more diverse people?

Group size adaptations: None are necessary. This activity can be completed by an individual, a small group, or an entire congregation. If you are completing the exercise on your own, you may just want to record the answer to the questions by using different colored markers to make hash marks in your journal. Of course, you will not be able to complete the portion of the bead exercise in which the group combines beads in one bowl. While recording your responses in your journal, however, you may decide to reflect on what you think the bowl would look like if your small group or church completed the exercise.

Exercise 21: Circle of Control
Prep Work Required: 10 minutes
Cost of Activity: None
Length of Time: 10 to 20 minutes

Materials

- a copy of *Portable Faith*
- a sheet of copy paper and a writing implement for each participant

Instructions

1. Read the following excerpt from the book *There Are No Children Here* as an individual or aloud as a group:

> *On June 13, a couple of weeks after their peaceful afternoon on the railroad tracks, Lafayette celebrated his twelfth birthday. Under the gentle afternoon sun, yellow daisies poked through the cracks in the sidewalk as children's bright faces peered out from behind their windows. Green leaves clothed the cottonwoods, and pastel cotton shirts and shorts, which had sat for months in layaway, clothed the children. And like the fresh buds on the crabapple trees, the children's spirits blossomed with the onset of summer.*
>
> *Lafayette and his nine-year-old cousin Dede danced across the worn lawn outside their building, singing the lyrics of L. L. Cool J rap, their small hips and spindly legs moving in rhythm. The boy and girl were on their way to a nearby shopping strip, where Lafayette planned to buy radio headphones with $8.00 he had received as a birthday gift.*
>
> *Suddenly, gunfire erupted. The frightened children fell to the ground. "Hold your head down!" Lafayette snapped, as he covered Dede's head with her pink nylon jacket. If he hadn't physically restrained her, she might have sprinted for home, a dangerous action when the gangs started warring. "Stay down," he ordered the trembling girl.*
>
> *The two lay pressed to the beaten grass for half a minute, until the shooting subsided. Lafayette held Dede's hand as they cautiously crawled through the dirt toward home. When they finally made it inside, all but fifty cents of Lafayette's birthday money had trickled from his pockets.* (Alex Kotlowitz, *There Are No Children Here* [New York: Anchor, 1992], 9.)

2. Instruct participants to draw a circle about the size of the mouth of a coffee cup on their paper. This circle represents

Dede's surroundings—the context in which she is being raised. Based only on the information presented in this story, instruct them to draw a circle inside the larger one representing how much control they estimate that Dede has over her surroundings.

3. Now instruct participants to draw a second circle the size of the mouth of a coffee cup next to Dede's. This one represents their context, including where they live, the resources they do or do not have, support systems, and so on. Then instruct participants to draw a circle inside that one that represents, on an average day, how much control they believe they have over their environment.

4. Looking at the inner control circles, how do they compare? Did you make them the same size? Is one bigger than the other? Explain why. If you're participating with a group, feel free to let others disagree or debate. If you are working on this exercise alone, try to imagine how someone might argue with your answer. Could someone create a case for taking the opposite side?

5. What if Dede had been a teenager or an adult in the story? How, if at all, would you change the size of her circle? Those who would change the size of the circle should share why they would change it so that everyone in the room can benefit from hearing a variety of opinions.

   Group size adaptations: You may decide to do this in combination with the film exercises, for example, using the movie based on the book this passage was excerpted from, which is also titled *There Are No Children Here*. Since the film was made for TV, it will likely not be available locally, so plan in advance to acquire it online.

Exercise 22: What They Deserve
Prep Work Required: None
Cost of Activity: $0
Length of Time: 20 to 60 minutes

Materials

- a copy of *Portable Faith*

Instructions

1. Pretend someone has asked you to be part of the team that will set the guidelines for the way in which welfare is distributed in the United States. What requirements would you put in place?

   Answer the questions on an individual basis first. Then you will be asked to submit ideas to the group. Here are areas to think about:

   - Who is eligible? Citizens? Noncitizens?
   - Do recipients need to be unemployed? Employed?
   - If they need to be employed, how much do they need to work? Part-time? Full-time?
   - Do they need to undergo some kind of job training or engage in a job search?
   - Are there any special exceptions for single mothers? What about pregnant women?
   - Do certain groups automatically qualify? Children? People with disabilities?
   - Would recipients need to be tested for drugs periodically?

- If recipients made too much money, they would obviously be ineligible. For a family of one adult and two children, how much is too much? At what point would you cut off their assistance?

- If this family of three had an income of eight hundred dollars per month, what amount of money would they need to make it through the month?

- Would you recommend that they be awarded the full amount you determined they need in the question above?

- Would you provide their assistance in cash, or would you provide some of it in food vouchers?

- What kind of accountability, if any, would you require to make sure the money is being spent on things that benefit the family?

- Is there a limit to how many consecutive months someone can receive assistance?

- Is there a limit to how many total, combined months someone can receive assistance in his or her lifetime?

- Does the limit apply to children? People who are disabled? Pregnant women?

- Would you provide health care to the family of three described above?

- Would you provide a day care stipend?

- Would you provide tax breaks?

- Would you provide grants or loans to individuals who wished to go to college?

2. Meet with the others in your group, and share your opinions on the questions above. Try to arrive at a compromise or a consensus for each question. Even though the exercise is hypothetical, if you are comfortable please share your opinions and stand up for the requirements you think would serve

our country best. The point is not to immediately agree but to draw out different perspectives on the topic so participants can learn from one another.

3. In coming to a consensus about welfare eligibility and how to distribute assistance, which questions were easiest to agree upon? Which were hardest? Were you challenged to reevaluate your perspective by someone else?

4. Pick a question that provoked different opinions or heated debate. Why do you think the issue was difficult to resolve?

5. In the United States, the country is dominated by two primary schools of thought. One philosophy suggests it is society's responsibility to help individuals in need. The other suggests each individual should take responsibility for himself or herself. Which attitude did the people in your group lean toward? Did they agree or disagree? Did this make it harder to come to a consensus?

6. Read the following excerpt from the *Leadership Journal* article below:

People with a heart to serve others want to know that their gifts are invested wisely. . . .

A truly worthy poor woman: a widow more than 65 years old, . . . is a woman of prayer and faith; never asks anyone for anything. . . .

A truly worthy poor young man: has completed school, . . . diligently applies for jobs every day; . . .

A truly worthy poor young woman: has illegitimate children conceived prior to Christian conversion; is now celibate. . . .

I want to serve truly worthy poor people. The problem is they are hard to find. . . . Are any of us truly worthy? (Bob Lupton, "A Truly Worthy Poor," *Leadership Journal* [Fall 1991], www.christianitytoday.com/le/1991/fall/9l4025.html)

7. When you first started reading the article, before you could see where the author was going, what was your internal reaction? Did you find yourself agreeing or disagreeing with what he was saying?

8. What would you say was the author's motive in writing the article? What was his point? And did you agree with it? Why or why not?

Group size adaptations: If you are completing the exercises as an individual, you will obviously not be able to form a consensus about welfare criteria with others. However, try your best to imagine how someone else could build a case that argues the opposite of your opinion. It may be helpful for you to think of people you know who hold strong opinions—people who are extremely conservative or extremely liberal, who are extremely wealthy or who struggle to make ends meet. How might they agree or disagree with your opinions?

Exercise 23: News You Can Use
Prep Work Required: None
Cost of Activity: $0
Length of Time: 10 to 30 minutes

Materials

- several local newspapers—enough that there is one section for each participant to review—or access to local news websites by using computers or phones
- a copy of *Portable Faith*

Instructions

1. Pretend you are a sociologist who is trying to learn as much about your community as possible. Based on the stories you find in the newspaper—or if you're using the Internet, by browsing comments that readers leave online—try to answer the questions below. It may be tempting to use your opinion or knowledge if you've lived in the community a while, but the rule is that you may use only information you find in the city paper.

- Does the community seem to be politically liberal, conservative, or moderate?

- Does the community seem to have a strong religious tradition? If so, can you tell what religions might be practiced or valued?

- What types of people does the community seem to look up to?

- What hobbies do people in the community seem to have? Is there any evidence of what they do recreationally (sports, boating, crafts, hunting, and so on)?

- What might people in the community fear? Is there evidence of crime and violence? Do the crime and violence impact the whole community, or are they mostly contained to a certain part of town?

- Do residents seem happy or dissatisfied with the local school systems? Is education valued?

- What kinds of health issues do people in the community face or show concern about?

- Do people in the community seem to eat consciously? Do they diet? Is there any evidence of interest in organic, vegetarian, or vegan meals?

- Is there any indication about what the community's workforce is like? What industries are dominant, for example? And is unemployment high or low?

- Do there seem to be hot button political or social issues that create controversy among residents?

- Do residents seem generally satisfied with the city or county government?

- What places tend to be local gathering spots? Malls? Parks? Stadiums?

- What events seem to attract a lot of local residents?

2. Did your findings, using the newspapers or websites, match up with your experiences and impressions of your community? Why or why not?

3. Do you get the sense that the reporters are likely from a similar race and economic or educational background as you, or would you guess they have a different background? Do you think this would influence you to agree or disagree with the way the staff reports the issues?

4. Is it possible that one person reading the newspaper could agree with a story, say, a story that suggests rising threats to public safety regarding crime, while another person could disagree? What about a reader's experiences or background might cause him or her to agree with a story about rising public threats? What might lead her or him to disagree with the suggestion that the threat is rising?

5. Now bring in your opinions. Respond to the following statements with true or false:

1. _____ Our community is safe.

2. _____ There is ample opportunity in our community to get a job if you work hard at it.

3. _____ Residents of our community have access to acceptable quality health care.

4. _____ Our community streets and public spaces are kept clean and litter free.

5. _____ There is ample opportunity to participate in sports or physical recreation in our community.

6. _____ There is ample opportunity for entertainment in our community.

7. _____ Our community offers children a quality education.

8. _____ Our community has jobs that pay well.

9. _____ Our community has an adequate amount of support services (such as police, fire, mental health services, and so on).

10. _____ Police in our community are responsive and fair.

11. _____ Judges in our community are consistent and fair.

12. _____ Residents of our community maintain their homes.

13. _____ Our community is not significantly affected by problems related to substance abuse.

14. _____ Parents in our community are responsible and nurturing.

6. After marking your answers, share them with others in the room. Are there people who live in the same community but answered questions differently from the way you did? Why? If everyone in the room is in general agreement, are there residents in the community who might disagree with all of you? Why?

7. Who would be likely to agree with number 10? Who might be likely to disagree with number 10? Why? What about number 5? Number 2?

   Group size adaptations: None are necessary. This activity can be completed as an individual, a small group, or an entire congregation. If you are completing the exercise as an individual, you may want to record your responses in your journal.

Exercise 24: Belief Web
Prep Work Required: 10 minutes
Cost of Activity: $0 to $20
Length of Time: 10 to 60 minutes

Materials

- a couple sheets of copy paper and access to several different colored writing implements for each participant
- a copy of *Portable Faith*

Instructions

1. People acquire beliefs through exposure to ideas and experiences. Because every person's life unfolds differently, every person has a unique web of ideas that inform beliefs about life, society, purpose, and so on.

   - family (parents or other relatives)
   - neighborhood
   - school

- community
- country
- workplace, field, or industry
- religion (church or faith group)
- information (reading, conferences, lectures, and so on)
- political party
- group affiliation (the military, the Kiwanis Club, the Boy Scouts, the Girl Scouts, and so on)
- life experience
- other: _____

2. Draw a circle the size of a quarter in the middle of the page. Write your name in the circle. Now add lines going out from the circle (like the rays of the sun). You will need one line for each group noted above that influenced you. Keep in mind you may need more than one line for groups with which you've been affiliated. Label each line with the name of a group listed above.

3. Now, going out from the group, try to include beliefs you acquired from each group. You will likely be able to identify several beliefs for each category.

Think about the following areas:

- Government (For example, on the family line, one line might say, "Be suspicious of government interference in our lives.")
- People of other races (For example: on the family line, it might say, "Avoid the south side of town.")
- Education (For example: on the school line, it might say, "You can get a good job only if you go to college.")

- Work (For example: on the political party line, it might say, "If people don't work, they shouldn't eat.")

- Politics (For example: on the workplace line, it might say, "Support the candidates who support the unions.")

- Religion (For example: on the information line, it might say, "Tithe 10 percent.")

- Finances (For example: on the life experience line, it might say, "Don't max out your credit cards.")

- Health (physical or mental) (For example: on the community line, it might say, "Work as much as you can to achieve the American dream.")

- Alcohol and drug use (For example: on the family line, it might say, "Drink responsibly, but avoid drugs.")

- Etiquette (For example: on the school line, it might say, "Wait your turn and hold doors for others.")

- Emotions (For example: on the family line, it might say, "Never cry in public.")

- Public appearance (For example: on the country line, it might say, "Be thin and always wear trendy clothes.")

4. When you are finished with your belief web, compare it to those of others. Is anyone's exactly the same as yours? Can you find someone with a similar belief on his or her web? Can you find someone whose web includes an opposite belief?

5. Discuss as a group the following:

- What sorts of things challenge our beliefs?

- When we encounter an experience that disproves our beliefs, we have several options: (a) ignore the evidence to the contrary and continue holding to the belief; (b) begin a search for new evidence to see if the belief might need to change, or (c) abandon the belief in favor of the new evidence. Which are you most likely to do?

- Do you know anyone who holds to his or her belief web without being willing to alter even one idea about an issue? What is the danger of such rigidity?

- Do you know anyone who too easily abandons personal beliefs without fully exploring the evidence? What is the danger of flip-flopping?

- Is it wise to spend time with people whose belief webs look entirely different from our own? Why or why not? What is the advantage of doing so? What is the disadvantage?

Group size adaptations: None are necessary. This activity can be completed by an individual, a small group, or an entire congregation.

Exercise 25: How the Spirit Moves
Prep Work Required: 5 minutes
Cost of Activity: None
Length of Time: 10 to 60 minutes

Materials

- several pieces of copy paper and a writing implement for each participant
- a copy of *Portable Faith*

Instructions

1. It can be difficult to talk about how the Holy Spirit moves in people or groups because of the range of thought on the

subject, but here are some ways that I or others have experienced what we perceived might be the Holy Spirit prompting us in our lives:

- Someone else, a speaker or a friend, spoke truth or insight into our situation in a way that helped us a great deal or gave us new direction. (For example, a counselor told us about a college sociology program that might interest us, and even though we'd never heard of sociology, we explored it and discovered our new career as a result.)

- We got a strong, difficult-to-explain internal sense that we should or should not do something. (For example, we felt compelled to buy a coat for a teen who seemed to need one. Or we felt compelled to speak words of comfort to someone who had lost a loved one.)

- We felt guilt over something we were about to do, were doing, or had done. (For example, our decision to tell a friend's secret troubled us.)

- We had a strong sense of peace about some action or idea after praying or spending time in reflection. (For example, we decided to resign from a job and pursue a different opportunity that presented itself.)

- While working or having a conversation with a person or a group, we experienced synergy and ideas, and energy came together in a new, insightful way. (For example, we determined that owning too many items infringed on our ability to enjoy life.)

- A specific idea or topic would not leave us alone. It kept recurring and appearing everywhere we went. (For example, we kept thinking about gang violence in our city. Then we saw a movie about it, ran into someone who started a ministry, stumbled onto a book written by a former gang member, and couldn't fall asleep at night without thinking about what could be done to prevent teens from being lured into gangs.)

- While we were reading, studying the Bible, painting, writing, or otherwise creating, ideas and thoughts readily flowed to us, seemingly providing us with ideas we'd never thought of before. (For example, we read a verse on poverty or saw how Jesus interacted with someone, and it changed the way we wanted to live or prompted us to make a new choice.)

- We got a strong sense that something we were doing or had just done was the way it should be. Something about it was just right. (For example, we worked with a group of kids in an after-school program one year and went home excited. We still feel bonded and good about the experience even now.)

- We had a strong emotional reaction (good or bad) to something we witnessed or experienced. (For example, we became incredibly angry when someone suggested that all kids have the same opportunity in life.)

- Other: _____

2. Make a time line of your life that begins with early childhood and ends with the present day. You may want to split the time line into sections for each decade of your life. For example, if you are fifty years old, you may split the line into five sections.

3. Spend time reflecting prayerfully on the time line you've just drawn. Draw hash marks that represent times of learning or revelation in your life, which may or may not have been from God. Use the list under item 1 to get ideas for the kinds of events to include.

4. Look for patterns in your answers. In reading the examples listed in parentheses above, for example, you may note that all of the following seem to reflect a similar theme:

- My interest in sociology had to do with understanding people, particularly youth, better.
- I decided to buy a coat for a teen in need.
- I could not shake my interest and concern for teen gangs.
- I was moved by a verse about our response to the poor.
- I really enjoyed working in an after-school program.
- I got angry when someone suggested that all kids have the same opportunity.

All of these suggest an ongoing passion for supporting disadvantaged teens.

If there are no patterns in your time line, check the hash marks you added, and look for one or two that stand out, or evoke a stronger emotional reaction in you, than the others.

5. Consider whether the pattern or labels you've identified may provide direction for a way to live your faith in the public sphere or a way to serve your community as either an individual or a church. For example, a person who has responded with the answers listed in number 4 might determine to mentor a teenager in the community or become a foster parent.

   Group size adaptations: None are necessary. This activity can be completed by an individual, a small group, or an entire congregation. If you are completing the exercise on your own, you may want to record your responses in your journal.

Exercise 26: Self-guided Neighborhood Tour
Prep Work Required: 20 minutes
Cost of Activity: $0 or cost of copies
Length of Time: 30 minutes recommended

Materials

- printed copies of "Self-guided Neighborhood Tour" from this exercise (1 copy per person)

Instructions

1. Copy the included "Self-guided Neighborhood Tour" (pages 154–155), and provide each person with one copy to help direct his or her observations as groups walk.

2. You may choose to have your entire group visit multiple neighborhoods over time, or you may divide the city among groups by assigning one neighborhood to each pair or group of three or four persons.

3. Encourage people to walk neighborhoods in groups of two or more, carry a cell phone, and be as minimally invasive as possible. Walking in broad daylight is preferable. Every neighborhood, including well-to-do and underprivileged communities, has a mix of friendly, helpful residents and those who perhaps appear unwelcoming. As a rule, it is best for participants to greet residents they meet and continue walking down the street. The goal here is to study the neighborhood. In later exercises, there will be more interaction.

   That said, God may prompt a group to talk at greater length with neighborhood residents. In this case, encourage people to use common sense. It is usually best not to enter unfamiliar homes, for example.

4. Instruct participants to take notes as they go. However, you might caution them that in situations where neighborhood residents are close by they may do well to put the sheets of paper for note-taking in their pockets and take notes later, when they are alone. Otherwise neighborhood residents could misunderstand why they are taking notes.

   Group size adaptations: None are necessary. This activity can be completed by an individual, a small group, or an entire congregation. If you are completing the exercise on your own, you may want to record your responses in your journal.

Self-Guided Neighborhood Tour
From *Portable Faith* by Sarah Cunningham.
Copyright © 2013 by Abingdon Press.

As you walk around the community, try to observe the unique qualities of each neighborhood. Do some neighborhoods have basketball hoops in nearly every driveway, while others have an abundance of bird feeders, for example? And what might these differences reflect? For instance, a neighborhood with sporting equipment is probably home to families with children, while a neighborhood with bird feeders might be home to nature enthusiasts or older people.

The items noted below are examples of features that could help you think carefully about the lives of the residents:

- number of city-installed public trash receptacles
- condition of roads and sidewalks
- number of No Trespassing or Beware of Dogs signs
- condition of parks
- number and condition of streetlights
- number of vacant buildings or lots
- number of houses for sale
- types of advertisements displayed
- presence of alcohol or drug paraphernalia
- amount of wildlife
- presence of pleasing or unpleasing smells
- presence of pleasing or unpleasing sights
- number of cars passing through or in driveways/garages

- types of residences (e.g., apartments vs. single-family homes vs. condos vs. government housing vs. mobile homes)
- presence of security systems
- number of broken windows
- presence of litter
- number of pedestrians
- number of bus stops or subway stations
- condition of sewers/drainage systems
- presence of languages other than English (in speech or writing)
- presence of graffiti
- closeness to grocery store, post office, bank, drugstore, library, churches, restaurants, public offices, police and fire stations
- number of trees/amount of green space
- number of fences/physical boundaries

Questions for Reflection

1. Based on what you observed, do you think that residents of some neighborhoods are experiencing a better quality of life than residents of other neighborhoods? For example, would residents of some neighborhoods feel safer than residents of others? Were some neighborhoods more visually appealing than others? How might people's impressions of the city and society be affected by where they live?

2. Did every neighborhood seem to enhance the life of its residents? Did all the neighborhoods present the same opportunity for self-sufficiency? For example, were basic goods and services available within walking distance, or were these establishments easily accessible via car or a bus route?

Exercise 27: Where We Drive
Prep Work Required: None
Cost of Activity: Cost of gas
Length of Time: 60 minutes

Materials

- 1 car per 2 to 4 people
- community map
- a copy of *Portable Faith*

Instructions

1. When communities are first coming together, roads are laid to allow residents to travel from place to place within the area. Roads must reach every house and business, connecting them in a grid, web, or other system of streets.

   - What would you consider the main residential and commercial roads (excluding highways) in your community? Which roads are most commonly used by the most people to get to where they're going?
   - Which roads—either specific street names or types of roads—would you estimate are least used?
   - Which residential areas would you consider the most populated?
   - Which residential areas are the least populated?

2. Over time, as areas become more populated, they are often connected to larger state or interstate highways to enable faster travel between commonly visited destinations. These

roads allow cars to move at a fast speed without traveling through residential neighborhoods with low speed limits, stop signs, streetlights, bicyclists, and pedestrians, which may require frequent stopping.

- What major highways exist in your community?

- Obtain a detailed map of your community that shows the street names in residential areas. Circle neighborhoods that are being bypassed by highways, which you would otherwise have to travel through.

Go out in pairs or groups, and purposefully visit these neighborhoods to expose yourself to the networks of people and places that are part of your community. Drive through your community, looking for neighborhoods and neighbors you don't often see or you've never taken the time to see before.

3. Discuss the following questions:

- Did you observe any areas you'd never been to?

- Were you surprised by any features of the area that you did not expect?

- Some might suggest that when we avoid certain neighborhoods either purposefully or just to use roads that offer more convenience or speed, we live detached from some of our fellow residents. Do you think there is truth in this? Why or why not?

- In relationship to this idea, some might suggest that it is easier for us to live detached from the needs of others when we don't have regular exposure to them—that we can almost forget them and their needs. Do you think this is true? Why or why not?

Group size adaptations: None are necessary. This activity can be completed by an individual, a small group, or an entire congregation. If you are completing the exercise on your own, you may want to record your responses in your journal.

Exercise 28: For a Day
Prep Work Required: 20 minutes
Cost of Activity: $0
Length of Time: Minimum, 1 day

Materials

- varies

Instructions

1. Sometimes we struggle to understand or be compassionate toward people whose lives, challenges, and needs are different from our own. As a result, it can be eye-opening to spend some time empathizing with groups and attempting to understand what it's like to walk in their shoes. Choose an upcoming day to try to experience a small part of what it is like to be someone with different needs from yours. Some ideas might include the following:

- Volunteer to help or job-shadow someone who does manual labor, works in a food kitchen, or has some other job that requires physical effort or could possibly have a stigma attached to it.

- Fast out of solidarity with people who don't have enough to eat.
- Fast out of solidarity to understand.
- Go everywhere you need to go in a day using public transportation or walking.
- Use crutches, a cane, or a wheelchair.
- Sleep outside on a cold night.
- Spend a week living on the budget of a person under the poverty line.
- Watch your children or someone else's for twenty-four hours without assistance from your spouse or a third party.

2. Write an essay or reflection on what it was like to see the community through another person's eyes, and share it with an individual, a group, or your social network or blog readers.

   Group size adaptations: None are necessary. This activity can be completed by an individual, a small group, or an entire congregation. If you are completing the exercise on your own, you may want to record your responses in your journal.

Exercise 29: Walking Tour
Prep Work Required: 3 to 6 hours
Cost of Activity: Cost of gas
Length of Time: 30 to 60 minutes

Materials

- the Internet, local library, or access to other reference materials about your community

- a car or a van suitable for driving others

Instructions

1. Develop a walking or driving tour of your community. Start by learning the history of your city. Look for information about the following:

  - the history of your city's or county's name—why was the name chosen, what does the name mean, and did the name change at all over time?
  - city population:
  - the origins of the county that encompasses your city:
  - stories about the first settlers to come to your area:
  - your town's participation in political and social movements:
  - the organization of your community's governments (city and/or county):
  - major industries:
  - historical monuments:
  - prominent or unique buildings:
  - demographics (age, race, income level, and so on of population):
  - schools and rivalries:
  - churches:
  - colleges and universities:
  - residents' or area's involvement in wars or other historical events:
  - famous people who were born or lived in the community:

- contributions to society, such as items invented by residents of your city:

- tragedies that have affected residents, especially large groups of residents, over time (fires, natural disasters, epidemics, and so on):

- riots or protests involving residents of the community:

- unique architecture:

- movies filmed in the community:

- residents' terms for various sides of town, nicknames:

- tourism spots where nonresidents visit:

- cuisine:

- sports:

- economy:

- law and government:

- sister cities:

2. Select a paragraph or two of interesting information about ten topics. Attach each topic to a location. For example, you could attach information about the area's founders to a particular road on the south side of town.

3. Don't just collect random information about the area, such as the height of a building. Look for stories that show personality and might be of interest to a listener. For example, you could say of a particular street on the city's south side, "Ironically, when this area was first settled, most people did not believe this part of town could be used for residential purposes because it was considered marshland. This allowed one man, Isaiah Root, to buy up two hundred acres in this area at an extremely low price, and he then divided the land into lots. He and his family lived in the first home he built, a large colonial, to prove to the community that the land was

habitable. After that, he made a nice profit in selling individual lots. Root's new subdivision was so successful that he gained a reputation across the city as an entrepreneur and was later elected mayor. In fact, Root Street is named after Isaiah."

4. Practice rehearsing the information until you memorize it. Or if you are not able to memorize it, make note cards with key information printed on them.

5. Deliver the tour to at least one group of people, so you can practice orienting people to thinking about and celebrating your community. You may even be able to use the tour in some type of small-group or ministry training or in a new membership orientation for your church to stress your church's emphasis on building relationships in the community. Another idea would be to use the tour as an in-house fund-raiser for a youth group outing or missionary or charitable event. Invite those who go on the tour to pay a small fee or to make a donation to the cause.

Group size adaptations: None are necessary. This activity can be completed by an individual, a small group, or an entire congregation.

Exercise 30: Taste of Your Community
Prep Work Required: 30 minutes
Cost of Activity: Cost of paper products and drinks plus $5 for each participant
Length of Time: 2.5 to 3 hours

Materials

- index cards
- paper plates
- optional: public transportation map

Instructions

1. Divide the group into pairs or small groups.

2. Give each pair or group an index card bearing the name and location of an area restaurant.

3. When you make the cards, purposefully include restaurants that span a wide variety of ethnic foods as well as restaurants that are located in different parts of town. Intentionally include parts of town that your average church attender might not usually visit.

4. As an option, you could require groups to travel by foot or public transportation only. If your area does not have public transportation, participants could drive. Additionally, you could make a rule that they are not allowed to use the Internet or the phone to find directions. They have to do it the old-fashioned way and ask residents for directions. Doing this gives them broader exposure to the local culture.

5. Each pair or group should spend five dollars per person on foods from their assigned restaurant. They should be encouraged to ask which menu items are house specials or local favorites and seek to purchase at least a sampling of these items.

6. Pairs or groups should return to the church or a designated meeting spot in the community (such as a park if the weather permits). Spread out the food buffet style, slicing entrées into sample sizes so that group members can get a taste of the food offerings available in your city.

7. Ask groups to share their experiences. Questions might include the following:

- Did you visit a place you had never been or rarely go to?

- Did you at any point feel uncomfortable, for example, as if you were attracting attention as outsiders?

Did they have interesting experiences or make insightful observations at the restaurant or when traveling in the community?

Group size adaptations: To do this activity as an individual, if you can afford it, you could invite a friend to tag along and stage a progressive dinner, where you eat an appetizer at one restaurant, a salad or soup at the next, an entrée at the next, and dessert at the last. If this is cost prohibitive, you could visit the restaurants just to see the buildings and ask for a to-go menu, so you can see what kinds of entrées are available. After collecting all the menus, if you have the money and time, you could then choose one to visit for dinner. You may want to record your responses to the questions noted above in your journal.

Exercise 31: Bus Ride
Prep Work Required: 10 minutes
Cost of Activity: Bus fare
Length of Time: 1 to 2 hours

Materials

- a copy of *Portable Faith*

Instruction

1. The groups should meet at a bus or subway terminal in your community.

2. Each group should be given a different destination, and they must use only public transportation. (All the assigned des-

tinations should be different, but they should be within a couple of blocks or so of each other so the group can reconvene in a public place such as a restaurant or a park.) Group members must use posted maps or ask transportation staff members or other people to determine their routes. Their goal is to reach the destination as quickly and affordably as possible.

3. As they are riding, group members should try to observe the unique characteristics of public transportation systems, particularly comparing public transportation to driving.

4. All groups should reconvene at a preappointed spot.

5. Discuss the following:

- How easy or difficult was it to determine the route? Was information about rates and fares easily accessible?

- Did you succeed in catching the right combination of buses or trains the first time, or did you make mistakes (miss a bus or train, go in the wrong direction, and so on)?

- How did the time it took to travel via public transportation compare to the time it would take to travel between the same places by car?

- What challenges did you notice might be present when riding public transportation that are not present when traveling by car?

- Which residents might experience the most hardship when using public transportation?

- Were the route times or destinations convenient for workers on day shifts? Afternoons? Night shifts? What if someone wanted a ride to area churches on a Sunday? Are there routes to get them there affordably?

Group size adaptations: This activity can be completed by an individual, a small group, or an entire congregation. If you complete it alone, however, you will have to select an address to visit by yourself rather than be part of a group that goes out in pairs to various addresses. You may want to travel during the day and sit close to the driver to increase your comfort and safety if you ride alone.

Exercise 32: Laundry
Prep Work Required: 10 minutes
Cost of Activity: $10 per person or per pair of people
Length of Time: 2 to 3 hours

Materials

- index cards
- dirty laundry
- detergent

Instructions

1. Divide the larger group into pairs.

2. Provide each pair with an index card bearing the name and address of a Laundromat in the area. Purposefully choose Laundromats that are spaced out so that participants can go to various places around town.

3. Instruct group members to do their laundry at the Laundromat and to interact with and observe others as they do so.

4. After they finish doing the laundry, reconvene in a group meeting spot, or wait until the next group meeting to share reflections.

5. Discussion points may include these:

- Who was doing laundry? Did it appear to be single people? Families? Single moms? Older people? A variety of people?

- Did you get the sense that people were doing laundry because they did not have a washer and dryer in their home? Or did you notice someone who chose to do laundry at the Laundromat for convenience or speed (for example, a baseball coach washing uniforms for the Little League team, a homemaker washing comforters too big for a standard household washing machine, a bachelor who had stored up mountains of laundry and wanted to complete it all at once rather than wash one load at a time).

- How did people get the laundry there? Did they cart it in a car? Did they walk it over or bike it over in bags or baskets?

- Did anyone bring children to the Laundromat? How did this change the task at hand?

- What did people do while waiting for the laundry to finish? Did they browse waiting room magazines, play on their phones, make small talk?

- Did people in the Laundromat seem to interact easily? Why or why not?

- Did the Laundromat seem safe? If you were doing laundry there at night, would you feel equally safe?

- Is there anyone who would experience more challenge in doing laundry at this facility?

Group size adaptations: None are necessary. This activity can be completed by an individual, a small group, or an entire congregation. If you are completing the exercise on your own, you may want to record your responses to the questions in your journal.

Exercise 33: Possessions
Prep Work Required: None
Cost of Activity: $0
Length of Time: Varies

Materials

- a copy of *Portable Faith*

Instructions

1. Some people believe that when you own more possessions than you need or can use, you are stealing from those who need them. Another way of saying this is that when God gives us more than we need, God is appointing us to distribute the excess to those in need.

2. What are some reasons that we may accumulate more than we need? Circle the reasons below that apply to you. Write in additional reasons not listed that may be unique to your situation. Discuss which reasons are most logical vs. which reasons may be illogical.

   Reasons for accumulating too much:

   - "I might need this later."

   - "It makes me feel good about my status or success to own all of this."

   - "I like having variety and being able to make choices."

   - "This reminds me of a good memory. I can't bear to part with this."

   - "I keep this because I think it somehow prepares me or protects me."

   - "This item is a reminder of my success. I keep it to prove to myself or others that my life is interesting or my career is successful."

- "People just keep giving me stuff, and I don't get rid of it."
- "I'm a compulsive shopper."
- Other: _____

3. What are the reasons it might be freeing to reduce the amount of possessions we own? Circle any reasons that are compelling or inviting to you. Write in additional reasons not listed that may be unique to your situation. Discuss which reason is most attractive for reducing the amount of possessions you own.

   Reasons for reducing the amount of possessions:
   - "I don't enjoy having to maintain these items" (e.g., washing, drying, ironing, folding, and so on).
   - "I don't have room to store everything I own, so my house feels cluttered."
   - "The more toys we have, the more toys my kids leave out on the floor."
   - "I don't use these."
   - "I have to make monthly payments or purchase insurance to own this."
   - "Other people may need these."
   - "Owning these items of value makes me feel vulnerable that someone might try to steal them."
   - Other: _____

4. Ask each group member to choose one of the following challenges for changing the way he or she owns possessions.
   - For two days, add up the amount of time you spend caring for or picking up possessions. Make a list of other things you could do with that time if you were able to cut the maintenance time in half.

- Walk around your house, and make a list of all the things you do not want or use, including the estimated value you might get if you sold them. Then total the value of your entire list (the amount you might receive if you sold all of it). Make a list of ways you might use that money for good, for yourself, your family, or someone in need.

- Pack a suitcase with all the clothing or entertainment items you need to live one week of your life. Then force yourself to get dressed and practice hobbies using only items in that suitcase for *two weeks*. It is okay to wash the clothes and reuse them. Does paring down your choices simplify your life or morning processes?

- Walk around your house, and place stickers on anything you haven't used in one month. Leave the stickers on the items. Over the next month, determine to use the items you have if you enjoy them. If you still have not used the items at the end of a month, resolve to throw away, donate, or sell them.

- Consider donating the same amount or a percentage of the amount to a worthy cause if you spend money on things you consider luxuries—a massage, a manicure, or an item at a high-priced store. In this way, you live with greater awareness that not everyone has the ability to purchase the things you do, and you express care for those who lack.

- Buy an outfit at a secondhand store, and incorporate it into your wardrobe.

- Sell clothes at a consignment store or a garage sale or on eBay, and give away the profits or at least a portion of the profits.

Group size adaptations: None are necessary. This activity can be completed by an individual, a small group, or an entire congregation.

Afterword

The curious thing about the seeds of this book is that they remained planted, both in me and in the church where I was on staff, even when the winds of change swept through.

After marrying, I left the church where the story behind this book began and moved with my husband to live alongside and teach urban teenagers in our city.

The church where all of this unfolded still stands, although it has undergone significant transition and is led by an almost entirely different staff team now. But although the face of the church and its outreach efforts has, of course, evolved, on every occasion I visit, my heart is warmed by the obvious enthusiasm the church has maintained for its community. Their people continue to carry Jesus—in their words, in their actions, in their beings—from their building to its surroundings. And the value of going is most definitely alive and well, if not more firmly embedded in the church's identity than ever before.

I too have moved on. This past summer, ten years later, my family moved out of the city to a nearby community and I moved into a whole new phase of mothering, writing, and speaking about these and other related topics at church communities across the country.

But life's sweeping changes only underline the steady, open-handed nature of the exercises contained here. They can, without a doubt, create an immediate swell of "going," but perhaps even more valuable is that they are then followed by a long tail of love and learning that still stirs people long after they've been completed. And the yearning they create does not demand building or maintaining a specific kind of outreach system for a specific length of time but only invites God to stir a lasting love for all people in all of us.

Now, as many of the staff I worked with have moved to other ministry efforts and even started their own churches, it delights me to know we are all still teamed with one another and with all of you who read in the same task. We remain pieces of a global church, taking Jesus to our own small corners of the planet we share.

My hope, then, is that the messy, bold, and zealous among you take courage to chase down the vision God stirs in you and to not give up until he brings it to expression in your community. In addition, I have high hopes that the leaders among you will come alongside the impassioned and eager, and help them learn to go with wisdom and grace, as many of those who imprinted my own life did.

Blessings on the noble and grand journey ahead.

CPSIA information can be obtained at www.ICGtesting.com
Printed in the USA
LVOW102339070313

323058LV00002B/3/P

9 781426 755156